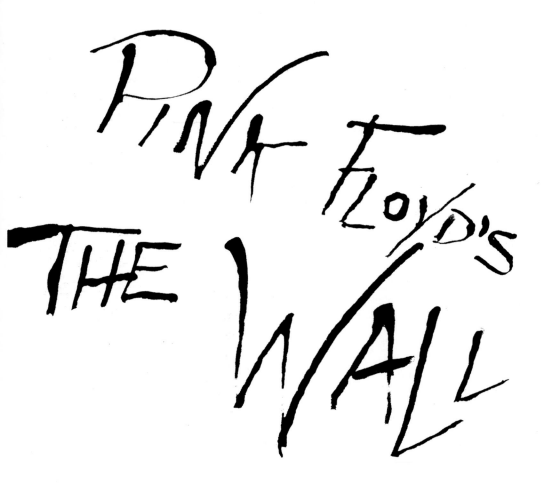

IN THE STUDIO, ON STAGE AND ON SCREEN

PINK FLOYD'S THE WALL

IN THE STUDIO, ON STAGE AND ON SCREEN

JEFF BENCH AND DANIEL O'BRIEN

Reynolds & Hearn Ltd
London

First published in 2004 by
Reynolds & Hearn Ltd
61a Priory Road
Kew Gardens
Richmond
Surrey TW9 3DH

A CIP catalogue record for this book is available from the British Library.

ISBN 1 903111 82 X

Designed by James King.

Printed and bound in Malta by Interprint Ltd.

CONTENTS

PREFACE

THE WALL IN CONTEXT

Anyone born in Britain late enough to miss the Swinging Sixties but early enough to witness the Gloomy Seventies will find that Pink Floyd's music provides a uniquely two-directional view and vision: back towards the era they missed, and forward into the era they experienced.

From the sunny, experimental climate of Swinging London to the emergence of Thatcherite politics and mass unemployment is a huge leap in social attitudes and creative opportunities. The Pink Floyd are arguably unique in being the only major British band to straddle these eras – and to have produced successful work in such differing social climates – while always remaining true to their roots in British pop and British culture. From the idyllic rural landscape of *Ummagumma*'s 'Grantchester Meadows' to the urban nightmare of 'Another Brick in the Wall' is a very long journey, but it is a journey that is thoroughly characteristic of Britain in the sixties and seventies. The rustic dreams of Britain's flower children, themselves part of the long tradition of back-to-the-land political movements and specifically English romantic idealisation of the countryside, seemed set to usher in a new, tolerant, post-industrial culture, of which the hippies and their part-time acolytes were the elite avatars. But this blissful future never arrived. Peace and love became a tired joke, and by the late seventies the new realities were economic dislocation and sporadic urban terrorism, spilling over from the conflict in Northern Ireland. Hippies were out. The punks had arrived, detesting everything which the hippies were held to represent.

Pink Floyd were there for the whole trip, from Carnaby Street to the Brixton riots. The band and their music encapsulates great changes in British society. One of their members became a casualty of the journey. Even their early work contains seeds of the menacing elements that were later to dominate ('Careful With That Axe, Eugene', 'One of These Days'). This book focuses on *The Wall*, the Floyd's classic album of 1979, as well as the Alan Parker movie of the same name. But ideally *The Wall* should be experienced in the context of all of Pink

Floyd's work: its cynicism, disillusionment and disgust with repressive elements in British society should seem more telling when viewed through the sombre lyricism of the Floyd's major early works such as 'A Saucerful of Secrets' or 'Echoes'. The sadness, the sense of public and private loss that haunts so many of Roger Waters' lyrics, is present from the very early days of the band. Through the seventies, this lyrical melancholy hardens into cynicism and then anger, through the album sequence *Dark Side of the Moon*, *Wish You Were Here*, and *Animals*.

Pink Floyd's music is a barometer of Britain's deteriorating mental health in the seventies. But their music is also a classic illustration of the constantly expanding musical horizons of that decade, a decade in which music maintained a position of importance in the general cultural life of the country which it does not enjoy today. To understand Pink Floyd's innovations in the longform rock track and the concept album, it is useful to go back much further, to the origins of the modern rock album itself. We should remind ourselves of the extraordinarily rapid evolution of pop music in the late sixties. This process was a true revolution in the means of artistic expression which the Floyd were heirs to. Having absorbed the developments taking place around them, the band were then instrumental in driving the evolution of rock to its next plateau of achievement.

ONE

FROM LP TO CONCEPT ALBUM

In the late 1940s, two new kinds of analogue disc were introduced into the record market. Both were to have an enormous impact on the future development of what became known as rock music. The two formats were, of course, the 45 rpm ('revolutions per minute') seven-inch single (introduced by RCA in 1949) and the 33 rpm 12-inch long-playing record (or LP), first marketed by Columbia in 1949. For most of the 1950s, for consumers throughout the world, these two new music formats continued to be manufactured and sold alongside the existing pre-war format, the ten-inch 78 rpm disc.

Initially, it was the 45 rpm single that had the greatest impact on pop music. The singles charts, populated by the ubiquitous seven-inch discs, became virtually synonymous with rock and roll and all its commercial chart derivatives. In bars and clubs worldwide, the little black discs were plucked automatically from the storage racks by robot armatures and slapped down on the turntables of Wurlitzer juke boxes, each one becoming, for a brief two minutes or so, 'The Record Now Playing'. The 33 rpm album, with its longer, 15 minutes plus playing time per side, was slower to make a major impact on the pop industry. The singles charts were the charts that mattered. Albums were an expensive purchase for the target teenage market, and most fifties albums played it safe, consisting of a collection of familiar hits and filler tracks. And it was only artists with a successful track record in the singles charts who made albums at all. If an album had any thematic concept, it was of the straightforward variety, such as Elvis Presley's *Elvis' Christmas Album* of 1957.

Jazz musicians, however, with their established traditions of extended improvisation, soon began to take advantage of the additional playing time afforded by the LP format. From the mid-fifties onwards, it becomes apparent that the creative processes of jazz as recorded music and the structure of recording sessions themselves were being shaped by the possibilities of the 12-inch LP. Aimed at an older target market with (in theory) greater disposable income, jazz albums could fit four, five or six extended improvisational pieces onto their two sides. The significance of this fifteen-minutes plus playing time soon became part of the nomenclature itself: jazz albums being referred to as 'sides'.

For example, Miles Davis' groundbreaking 1948 *Birth of the Cool* recording sessions have been endlessly repackaged and discussed as if they constituted an album. But these classic sessions were conceived to provide material for a series of 78 rpm singles – only subsequently were the individual tracks collected together on a 12-inch LP, and treated as a single recording. Davis' renowned 1954 sessions with the Modern Jazz Giants were at first released by Prestige on yet another format, a ten-inch, 16 rpm album – an unusual format for music, more normally employed at that time for spoken-word recordings. This album was re-released in 1956, with a slightly different selection of tracks, as a 12-inch LP. Both 16 rpm and 33 rpm versions include the two eight-minute-plus takes of 'The Man I Love'. 'The Man I Love (take one)', sequenced at the end of the 33rpm album's second side, even incorporates a false start to the performance, and a subsequent snatch of acerbic dialogue between Davis and pianist Thelonius Monk. 'I don't know where to come in, man…' says Monk. He continues 'We're going to put these [false starts] on the record, all of them.' This incident, captured on record, spawned the legend that the two jazz giants had actually come to blows during the recording session, a myth which Ira Gitler's notes on the cover of the '56 re-issue are keen to dispel.

A trivial incident in jazz history, perhaps, but the greater space of 12-inch albums allowed for the first time the inclusion of false starts, snippets of studio dialogue and other material extraneous to the music itself. The tight limitations of the 78 disc had excluded such accidents and frivolities. The more relaxed attitude to the recording of these mid-fifties improvisation jazz albums contains the seeds of the self-aware attitude to the recording process that led to the extensive inclusion of studio dialogue and other non-musical material in the sixties recordings of Bob Dylan, Frank Zappa, The Beatles and many others. Coupled with the development of a new, distinctive style of artwork for album covers by jazz labels such as Prestige and Blue Note, this new attitude to recording and sequencing jazz performances signals the emergence of the 33 rpm LP format as a creative medium in its own right. The jazz album of the late fifties had become more than simply a technical specification in which to issue recorded music. It was an important cultural artefact, with many levels of resonance. In Marshall McLuhan's familiar phrase, 'the medium is the message'. Pop's medium was the single, the 'hot' medium of two-minute instant gratification. Jazz's empire was the 'cool' world of the album: sophisticated, meditative and unhurried.

So, as the 1950s drew to a close, it continued to be jazz musicians alone who enjoyed the flexibility and control of their recording dates and a marketing strategy from record labels which allowed albums to be released that were informed by a coherent creative intent. This coherent vision might be as straightforward as the specific assemblage of musicians involved. For example, Milt Jackson and Ray Charles' 1957 *Soul Brothers* or Lee Morgan and Hank Mobley's 1958 *Peckin' Time* are albums unified by a creative 'concept' only in the rudimentary sense that the performances included are specific to that collection of musicians playing together at that specific recording session. And, unlike almost all pop musicians of the fifties, Jackson, Charles and the rest were playing their own compositions, or their own arrangements of standards and show tunes. The hard bop classic *Art Blakey's Jazz Messengers with Thelonius Monk* is entirely typical of the era's approach to recording (and marketing) a jazz album. The major draw for the listener is the prospect of Blakey's driving, hard-bop drums (backed up by the rest of Blakey's outstanding Jazz Messengers) going up against the dissonant, syncopated 'plunkety-plunk' piano of Thelonius Monk. The tunes on which the quintet improvise on are mainly standard Monk compositions from the previous decade: 'Evidence', 'In Walked Bud', 'Blue Monk' and so on, with the inclusion of one composition ('Purple Shades') by tenor sax player Johnny Griffin. If there is a unifying design to this particular jazz album or the hundreds of others from the fifties and early sixties that resemble it in their basic circumstances, then this 'concept' lies in the choice of the musicians and the atmosphere of the session. Jazz musicians of the time referred to recording sessions as 'dates'. In the spirit of improvisation, whatever was played on that particular date became recording history – a one-off performance preserved for posterity on vinyl.

Miles Davis, as well as Milt Jackson and the rest of the Modern Jazz Quartet, were also closely associated with the so-called 'Third Stream' movement in fifties music. The Third Stream did not regard itself as a movement *within* the confines of jazz, but rather as an alternative to the clean split existing between classical orchestral music and jazz composition and performance practices. Miles Davis' Third Stream work is bound up with the trumpeter's collaborations with composer/arranger Gil Evans: in particular, *Porgy and Bess* and *Sketches of Spain*. *Sketches of Spain*, one of the key works in Davis' long and multi-facetted career, pitches Davis' soloing trumpet against Evans' atmospheric, understated orchestral counterpoint, creating a musical language and environment that is genuinely innovative. The unique feel of the music is sustained for the album's entire extent, which clocks in at over 40 minutes. But *Sketches of Spain* does not consist of one, continuous composition. Five separate pieces are included: Roderigo's 'Concierto di Aranjuez', De Falla's brief 'Will 'o the Wisp', and three Gil Evans' compositions: 'The Pan Piper', 'Saeta' and 'Solea'. Impressively,

Miles Davis

the overall effect of the album is not that of a selection of original compositions and covers, yoked together into some semblance of unity by Evans' skills as arranger and Davis' virtuoso trumpet work. Instead, the mood and the dynamic/harmonic unity of the five pieces builds into a whole greater than any sum of the parts. Yet this is a recording that lays no claim to being a single composition, being five different pieces by three different composers. The unifying principle is present at the level of the album's overall arrangement, the subtle mirroring and shifts of key from track to track, and what Nat Hentoff referred to as a 'brooding, dramatic Spanish sound.' The overall structure and the sequencing of the individual tracks might be said to resemble the structure of an orchestral suite, such as Holst's *The Planets*, while not having the melodic and harmonic unity of a full-blown symphony.

In fact, *Sketches of Spain* could lay a convincing claim to being the world's first concept album. The album proceeded from Davis and Evans' mutual decision to record an entire work in response to their shared appreciation of Roderigo's *Concerto di Aranjuez* for Guitar and Orchestra. Growing from this central idea, the entire album hangs together musically, but it also coheres as a narrative concept: it works as series of Spanish sketches. Unquestionably a high point of the Third Stream movement, *Sketches of Spain's* influence can be clearly heard in the orchestral movement in rock that commenced in the sixties and reached its apogee in the seventies. Davis and Evans's influence embraces such diverse recordings as The Beatles' *Sgt Pepper*, the orchestral version of The Who's *Tommy*, Santana's 'Every Step of the Way', The Moody Blues' *Days of Future Passed* and Frank Zappa's ventures into orchestrally-augmented versions of The Mothers of Invention, from *Lumpy Gravy* to *200 Motels* and beyond.

Sketches of Spain was released in 1960. At that date, the notion of an album as something more substantial than a collection of singles, b-sides, or 'fillers' had yet to gain acceptance in the world of pop. The Hollywood musical had its soundtrack albums, but these existed as an artistic unity only in relation to the movies from

GI blues – Elvis Presley in 1958

which they derived. For example, Elvis Presley's 1958 *King Creole* hangs together as more than a bunch of disconnected tracks only if one listens to it after watching the movie *King Creole*, the story based on Harold Robbins' *A Stone for Danny Fisher*. The title track 'King Creole' itself, 'Crawfish', 'Trouble', 'Steadfast, Loyal and True' and the rest of the songs only gel into some semblance of a narrative if we recall the points at which they occur in the movie (which is not the same order in which the album sequences them). Returning in 1960 from his two-year US Army posting in Germany, Elvis released what is arguably the most complete and unified album of his career: *Elvis is Back!* Everything about this release is subtly different from the old, pre-Army Elvis Presley. Something new is being presented, from the knitwear Elvis wears on the front cover, to the army snaps incorporated inside the (first ever?) gatefold sleeve, to the widely-varied musical genres from which the individual tracks are derived. All this signals a clear intention to produce a new kind of Elvis album that could consolidate the singer's position as The King, while moving his career forward into the new decade.

Sadly, this new-found energy and direction in Presley's recording career lasted for this one album only. But this should not blind us to the significant step forward that *Elvis is Back!* represented – for Presley, and for albums in general. Although Presley only received three song writing credits in his career, very few singers have been more adept at selecting material and shaping it to their own creative purposes. The content of *Elvis is Back!* is clearly chosen with the intent of mixing a wide variety of Elvis' styles, new and old, through which the singer showcased his range as a performer to both his established fans and the rising generation. The album weaves a number of musical threads into a complex whole, though not necessarily a whole that would be appreciated by all. John Lennon famously dismissed this and all subsequent Presley recordings with the curt judgement: 'Elvis sold out the day he joined the army.' In the sense that *Elvis is Back!* deliberately presents a new Elvis 'persona', the album prefigures the album-to-album shape-shifting of Bob Dylan in the 1960s and David Bowie in the 1970s. *Another Side of Bob Dylan, Highway 61 Revisited, John Wesley Harding; Young Americans, Station to Station, Low*: none of these are concept albums, but each one unveils a reinvented version of its creator. Not just a new style of music, but a new look, a new set of attitudes and a new persona that is startlingly different to the previous incarnation. As the poet Thom Gunn had written of Elvis Presley in 1957: 'Whether he poses or is real, no cat/Bothers to say.'

On *Elvis is Back!,* Presley attempts such a personal reinvention, perhaps the first of its kind. The album opens by putting the clock back to the pre-Army 1956-1958 sessions. The Jordanaires doo-whop their way through 'Make Me Know It', as they had through 'Don't Be

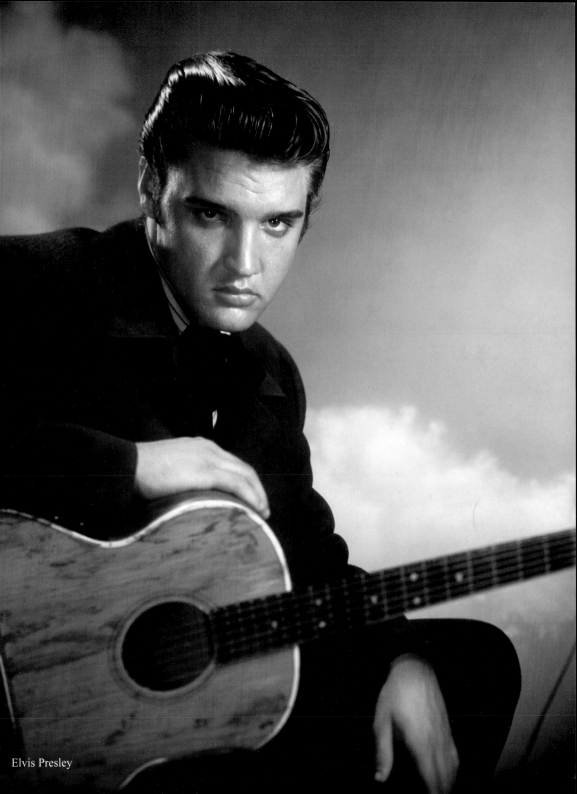

Elvis Presley

Cruel', 'Teddy Bear' and the rest of the 1956-58 recordings. Track two, 'Fever', slows the pace. Elvis sings this new standard in the Peggy Lee arrangement over plucked double bass and percussion – a new sound for an Elvis recording. 'The Girl of My Best Friend', in contrast, looks forward to the typical Elvis single of the early sixties: pleading, crooning vocals over a mid-tempo chord sequence from the rhythm guitar, with a cunning extra hook built into the middle eight. And so it goes on: recapitulation of the 'old' pre-Army Elvis ('Dirty, Dirty Feelin'', 'Such a Night'), catching-up with the pop's style changes in the missing Army years ('It Feels So Right') and premonitions of Elvis' sound of the sixties ('Girl Next Door Went A' Walking', 'Thrills of Your Love'). Mixed among these Elvis styles old and new, there are two additional elements. One of these is the introduction of 'autobiographical' songs that clearly play on Elvis' recent Army career ('I Will Be Home Again', 'Soldier Boy'). The other significant fresh element is the false dawn of Elvis as white Chicago Blues singer – a new persona unveiled on 'Like a Baby' and especially on the astounding climactic cover of Lowell Fulson's 'Reconsider Baby', served up complete with a raunchy Boots Randolph sax solo. There is a slyness about the way in which Elvis' various personas – the wide-eyed and horny redneck, the regular army dude, the night club sophisticate, the white blues singer – all slot neatly together, their underlying tensions effortlessly resolved by Elvis' all-conquering voice and lopsided, ironic grin. Elvis would not project himself so effectively again until his return to live performance in 1968. Although *Elvis is Back!* stands a long way from the notion of the concept album, its clever choice of material, the sequencing of the individual tracks, and the considered artistry by which the arrangements and instrumentation are varied across all 12 tracks all represent a new, more sophisticated approach to the recording of a pop album. *Elvis is Back!* is more than just 12 tracks pressed together: it succeeds on certain levels as a coherent whole.

Released in 1960, *Elvis is Back!* still belongs to the cultural landscape of the 1950s, an era in which the recordings of pop artists, even giants of Presley's stature, did not command the serious attention of the cultural mainstream. Rock and roll was perceived as a fad for teenagers, and any serious performer was expected to try to get into something else as soon as possible. (Elvis, and particularly his manager Colonel Parker, saw a better future in Hollywood). But as the 1960s began to unfold, winds of change began to blow through the enervated aftermath of the rock and roll era. Early signs appeared of what would become the British invasion. But the initial challenge to the major US labels' received wisdom of what might constitute a hit record formula came from the folk music revival. The folk movement as a commercial force was spearheaded by the likes of Joan Baez, Peter, Paul and Mary, The

Bob Dylan

PiNk Floyd's THE WALL

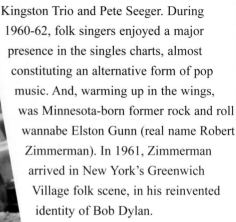

Kingston Trio and Pete Seeger. During 1960-62, folk singers enjoyed a major presence in the singles charts, almost constituting an alternative form of pop music. And, warming up in the wings, was Minnesota-born former rock and roll wannabe Elston Gunn (real name Robert Zimmerman). In 1961, Zimmerman arrived in New York's Greenwich Village folk scene, in his reinvented identity of Bob Dylan.

This is not the place to discuss or even outline the ways in which Dylan redefined first folk, then pop and then rock. Suffice to say that it was Dylan, together with The Beatles, who by 1964-65 had completely redefined the parameters of how a popular artist could approach the recording of an album. Dylan's first album, the eponymous *Bob Dylan*, is almost entirely made up of cover versions and traditional songs, in the established folk manner. It was Dylan's second album, *The Freewheelin'*, recorded in late 1962 and released in May 1963 that truly broke the mould. This remarkable album contains 13 songs, of which 11 are original Dylan compositions. *The Times They a Are A' Changin*, released in February 1964, completed the evolutionary process, with all ten tracks being Dylan originals.

Considered as a collection of songs, *The Freewheelin'* has a clear identity and a very clear set of intentions. Dylan's first album had not achieved great commercial success, though it had been generally well-received by the critics. *The Freewheelin'* sets out to establish Dylan's status as a singer-songwriter who stands head and shoulders above his contemporaries – Nat Hentoff's liner notes specifically make this claim on Dylan's behalf. The original Dylan songs included fall into clearly definable categories, and the lyrics reference from one song to another, sometimes frankly, sometimes ironically, to build up a diverse picture of Dylan's beliefs and preoccupations: political, social, artistic, emotional, erotic. Without repeating himself, Dylan picks up and restates particular themes from one song to another, sometimes in a very different context or emotional register. For example, the nuclear Armageddon which Dylan prophecies in 'A Hard Rain's A-Gonna Fall' is revisited in a very different mood of

go Starr, Paul McCartney, John Lennon
George Harrison – The Beatles in 1964

satire and burlesque in 'Talking World War lll Blues'. Likewise, the nostalgia which pervades 'Girl From the North Country' and 'Bob Dylan's Dream' and the lament for lost innocence which these songs embody is mercilessly burlesqued in the humorous squib 'I Shall Be Free'. The intense 'gotta travel on' blues persona of 'Down The Highway' is similarly undercut in the lightweight 'Bob Dylan's Blues'.

Such analysis as the above is inclined to make *The Freewheelin'* sound schematic in its structure: it is not. The album heralded the emergence of Dylan as the USA's best-known protest singer. The album's overtly political songs, such as 'Masters of War' and 'Oxford Town', gain hugely in impact from their juxtaposition with love songs such as 'Don't Think Twice It's All Right' and 'Corrina, Corrina' (the latter being one of the album's two non-Dylan songs). The opening song, the folk-movement anthem 'Blowin' In The Wind', sounds like a protest song itself, but, despite the protest-inspired imagery that infuses the lyrics, the song cannot easily be reduced to a statement about any particular institution or system. However, the song (and Dylan's performance) certainly captures the curious mixture of anger and nostalgia that runs through *The Freewheelin'* like letters through a stick of Brighton Rock. In contrast, Dylan's follow-up album, *The Times They Are a-Changin'*, fails to achieve the earlier record's level of creative unity, despite – or perhaps because of – its deliberately narrower emotional range. Uncompromisingly recorded and sold as Dylan's 'protest album' (the last album he would make as a recognisable part of that movement), *The Times They Are a-Changin'*, consists almost entirely of what Dylan himself referred to as 'finger-pointing songs'. Containing several of his strongest, most prophetic lyrics, in songs such as 'Only A Pawn In Their Game' and 'When The Ship Comes In', *The Times They Are a-Changin'* successfully *packages* Dylan as the folk-protest conscience of his generation. In that narrow sense, it is a step closer to the full-blown overt thematic unity of the concept albums of the late sixties and after. But considered as a unified work of art, displaying emotional shading and the effective blending of musical influences (folk, country, blues, rock and roll), *The Freewheelin'* is the more complex, more resonant and more successful whole.

The Freewheelin' almost succeeded in being the first album of entirely original material released by a pop artist. *The Times They Are a-Changin'* attained that goal. But Dylan, in 1963-64, was still effectively outside the world of charts, singles, and pop stardom. His only tailor-made single, 'Mixed Up Confusion'(1962) had sunk without trace, despite being recorded with a backing band which included guitarist Bruce Langhorne, who was to reappear on *Bringing It All Back Home*. Singles chart success and pop star status did not happen for Dylan until 1965, by which time the Beatles and the British Invasion of the US charts had blurred a number of boundaries.

The Beatles' first UK album, *Please Please Me* (1963), succeeded magnificently in translating the energy and originality of the band onto record. It also showcased Lennon and McCartney as songwriters (eight Lennon/McCartney songs are included). The album traversed a wide range of mood and style, from the unprecedented rawness of 'Twist and Shout' to the almost over-refined 'A Taste of Honey', and from the knowing bedside salsa of 'PS I Love You' to the naked emotion of 'There's A Place'. Even the Beatles' choices of non-originals broke the mould established by British artists: they only covered American soul, R&B and rock and roll hits, and played mostly songs popularised by black artists. The Beatles pointedly ignored the products of Britain's established Tin-Pan Alley tunesmiths, thus further indelibly stamping their early albums with their collective taste and iconoclasm. As with Elvis Presley, the impact of The Beatles as performers (live and on record) was so overwhelming to contemporary audiences, that the sheer emotional and musical range of their material tended to be taken for granted.

Nevertheless, working in collaboration with producer George Martin, each successive Beatles album shows an increasing sense of the LP format as a self-contained performance, requiring for its maximum impact intelligent selection, recording and sequencing of the material. At least, the original British releases reveal this development, less so the bastardised versions put out in the USA, with hit singles added, other tracks dropped, and running orders wilfully rearranged. *With The Beatles* (reworked as *Meet The Beatles* in the USA) is a similar, but stronger, confection to the first album. There are several obvious attempts to hit the same bullseyes as *Please Please Me*: 'Till There Was You' occupying the show tune role of 'A Taste of Honey', 'Money' replacing 'Twist and Shout' as the explosive R&B climax. There are seven Lennon/McCartney tracks, eight covers, and the first George Harrison song to be recorded, 'Don't Bother Me'. The Beatles' third album, *A Hard Day's Night*, released in July 1964, broke completely new ground by containing only original Lennon and McCartney songs. No other group was remotely this prolific in its creation of original material. Also unprecedented was the era-defining packaging of *A Hard Day's Night*. Its Warhol-influenced sleeve, featuring non-identical repeat images of the band members, created a new visual style for pop promotion which (for example) the credit sequence for *The Monkees* TV series shamelessly imitates.

The Beatles continued to produce groundbreaking singles throughout the remainder of 1964 and '65, including the first use of feedback on record ('I Feel Fine') and the radical rhythmic and harmonic experiments of 'Ticket to Ride'. While the Beatles ceaselessly developed their musical approach, they did not produce a second complete album of original songs until

Rubber Soul, released in November 1965. Signalling the beginning of the experimental phase that characterises the second half of the Beatles' career, *Rubber Soul* is a superb collection of original songs, brilliantly played, intelligently produced but sequenced in a slightly strange order. The album's unifying feature is its mood, which is (with certain notable exceptions) one of weary melancholy, laced with anarchic black humour. Recorded at the height of American Beatlemania, and in the wake of the sell-out Shea Stadium concert, *Rubber Soul*'s unexpectedly wry, sometimes almost nihilistic pessimism ('Norwegian Wood', 'Nowhere Man', 'Think For Yourself', 'Girl') is broken only by the promise of the transcending experience of love in 'The Word'. But the structure of the album leads one past this revelatory song, back into nostalgic yearning ('In My Life') and a statement of rejection ('If I Needed Someone') to the misjudged final track 'Run For You Life', which is unable to carry its abrasive burden of posturing cynicism. The relative emotional shallowness of 'Run For Your Life' fails to give *Rubber Soul* the kind of resonant conclusion which the qualities of the album as a whole deserve.

Rubber Soul's 14 tracks (as sequenced on the British version of the album) can at times seem like listening to a brilliant set of songs that have somehow been shuffled into the wrong order. Perhaps the Beatles and their producer were at some level unprepared for the heavy emotional weight of *Rubber Soul*'s material. The album stands a very long way from the hysterical, over-excited atmosphere that informs most of *Help!*, the bulk of which was recorded only months before. However, if one delves beneath the surface of *Help!*, the earlier album's lyrics also contain their own share of pessimism and despair. The title track 'Help!' itself is a case in point: taken on their own, the lyrics of this song paint a picture of near-suicidal despair, which the exuberance and energy of the song and the performance totally contradict.

The Beatles' next album, *Revolver*, set new boundaries to what might be possible within the context of a group recording an album. Long in the shadow of *Sgt Pepper*, *Revolver* is now firmly established as The Beatles' masterpiece. On several occasions it has also been voted the greatest album of all time. While not presenting itself as even a 'pseudo' concept album, as does the subsequent *Sgt Pepper*, *Revolver* might be said to break even more new ground than *Pepper*. Musically and lyrically innovative at many levels, *Revolver* also achieves an impressive level of focus and unity considered as a whole, despite the very wide range of emotions and musical styles which it embraces. 'Taxman', 'Eleanor Rigby' and the rest succeed magnificently as individual songs. But it is as an overall structure, a listening experience that embodies a genuine emotional journey, that *Revolver* is most relevant

The Beatles at
Abbey Road in
June 1967

to the subsequent emergence of the concept album. Whether by creative instinct or deliberate design, Beatles wrote and recorded a sequence of songs which document the individual's journey from spiritual despair to enlightenment. The currency of such words has been relentlessly debased in the years since the album first appeared, and it has also become unfashionable for any popular art form to attempt such lofty themes. *Revolver* achieves its ambitious aims with unobtrusive ease, leaving it entirely up to the listener to perceive, if they want to, the links that exist from song to song. So, allowing for the comic interlude of 'Yellow Submarine' and the romantic interlude of 'Here, There and Everywhere', the album moves from songs of materialism, isolation and death ('Taxman', 'Eleanor Rigby' and 'I'm Only Sleeping') to questioning songs ('Love You To', 'She Said, She Said') which paint everyday reality as an illusion and suggest an escape route from the nihilism of the first three songs. Side two (*Revolver* was of course conceived as a vinyl album, not a CD) opens with McCartney's optimistic hymn to diurnal happiness, 'Good Day Sunshine', and also embraces a despairing love song, 'For No One'. Love as we usually know it ('The Word') isn't enough anymore. The remainder of the album sets out the alternative paths to enlightenment: creativity ('And Your Bird Can Sing'), drugs (Dr Robert), and a form of mysticism ('I Want To Tell You'). The album concludes in a blazing, simultaneous acceptance of life as something precious to be savoured ('Got To Get You Into My Life') and as an illusion to be transcended ('Tomorrow Never Knows').

If *Revolver* has any deliberate unifying concept behind it, it is openly revealed only in the album's title. Influenced by George Harrison's investigations of Hindu philosophy (Harrison visited India for the first time in early 1966), the title of the album could refer to cycles of birth, death and reincarnation, the revolving 'wheel of dreams'. The album certainly moves from death and taxes towards some kind of spiritual rebirth, but the sardonic sensibility, which so often salvages the Beatles' work from the threat of pomposity, also supplies at least two punning double meanings. An LP record is 'a revolver', just as to be 'stuck in a groove' is a metaphor for boredom. And a revolver is also a kind of gun, with a revolving magazine in which each chamber carries a separate bullet – the preferred tool for playing Russian Roulette. If life and death are two sides of a pointless cosmic joke, *Revolver* invites us to laugh along with the amused Gods, not to cry out in loneliness and despair. Optimism on such a scale is perhaps the only aspect of *Revolver* which has dated since its release in August 1966.

Revolver may be the Beatles' high-watermark of artistic achievement, but is was the follow-up album *Sgt Pepper's Lonely Hearts Club Band* that finally alerted the cultural mainstream that something unprecedented was happening in the world of pop. *Revolver* broke the mould, but the more easily imitated *Pepper* opened the floodgates to album-length experimentation. There is nothing slyly subversive about *Sgt Pepper*: everything about it, from its Peter Blake cover design to its lyrics to its musical explorations, trumpet the notion that the world has now changed, and everything is now permitted. Although the psychedelic circus of *Sgt Pepper* does have its dark side ('She's Leaving Home') it is, nevertheless, an album almost completely free from the sour note of contempt for the 'square' world that infests 1968's *White Album*. *Sgt Pepper* is inclusive. Everyone, not just Billy Shears and his friends and LSD Lucy but also the nineteenth-century acrobat Mr Kite and Lovely Rita the authority figure are invited to the party. The conceptual window-dressing of the album – the costumes, the half-hearted attempt at linkages between some of the songs, the reprise of the 'Sgt Pepper' title track before the segue into 'A Day In The Life' – have ultimately much less bearing on *Pepper's* claim to be a unified work of art. The album's unity of conception derives from the Beatles' deep insight into the special moment in history at which the record was being produced: critic Ian MacDonald has elegantly described this as 'a cinematic dissolve from one zeitgeist to another'. The trans-generational optimism that *Pepper* embodies might be viewed as a utopian vision that has never come to pass. But it is at this level that the record achieves a thematic unity, a coherent creative vision which allows the kaleidoscope of songs, characters and styles to work together to create, in the mind of the listener, an integrated whole. Perhaps the strangest aspect of *Sgt Pepper* is that its outstanding concluding track, 'A Day In The Life', uses its every musical and lyrical device to puncture the optimism of the rest of the album. Yet somehow this sobering, deflating contemplation of the limitations of the everyday world does not undercut the party atmosphere of what has gone before. It's as if with 'A Day In The Life' the Beatles managed to repeat *Revolver's* achievement of standing both in- and outside mundane reality, and to infiltrate this Godlike posture without sacrificing their redeeming sense of humour.

'A Day In The Life' is one of the two longest tracks on *Sgt Pepper*, having a running time of five minutes three seconds. Despite the Beatles' enormous musical and lyrical innovations in the construction of their albums, their LP records up until 1967 still consisted of 12 or 14 more-or-less single-length tracks filling two sides of a 12-inch disc. By the mid sixties, other recording artists were brining about a further recording innovation which may seem trivial to us today, but should be seen as an essential step to the full-blown concept album. This innovation was simply the 'long' track: a track that lasted significantly more than five minutes.

Initially, three minutes had been the psychological barrier: the maximum playing time that could be squeezed onto a 45 rpm single. The Animals' single 'House of the Rising Sun' (1964) clocked in at almost five. Singles and album tracks were getting longer. It's easy to see increasing length as merely an excuse for repetitiveness, self-indulgence, or noodling guitar solos, and indeed it would be a futile labour to catalogue the amount of deliberate time-wasting perpetrated on vinyl from around 1965 onwards. But the freedom to record a song (or instrumental) that lasts more than three or five minutes is a fundamental building block necessary to working holistically on the larger canvas of the 40- or 50-minute album. The emergence of tracks lasting five, seven, ten, 12 or even 17 minutes (one whole side of an album!) signals a further break from the 1950s' notion of the pop album as collection of songs that couldn't quite make it as singles. For many bands, the achievement on record of a 'long' track seemed to amount to a recording rite of passage from the world of pop to rock – ie, in sixties' terminology, from triviality to seriousness of intent. Even the normally reticent Dylan was moved to remark on his own 1966 long track, 'Sad Eyed Lady of the Lowlands': 'Every record was more or less for impact. Why, I did one song on a whole side of an album! It could happen to anybody…'

In fact, it had been some of Dylan's mid-sixties musical collaborators who had led the way in the race to record longer tracks. Al Kooper (who plays on *Highway 61 Revisited* and *Blonde on Blonde*, as well as later Dylan albums) led his own band in the mid sixties, The Blues Project. The Project's first album included a 12-minute version of the traditional blues 'Two Trains Running'. The is one of the first extended white blues performances in which the running time of the song is lengthened by extended soloing in turn by various instruments, imitating part of the musical structure of modern jazz. Paul Butterfield's Chicago-based Butterfield Blues Band also provided several of the backing musicians for Dylan's first-ever amplified performance at the 1965 Newport Festival. In 1966, Butterfield's own band released their second album, which incidentally also includes a much shorter, three-minute version of 'Two Trains Running'. The album also features a 13-minute original composition, 'East West', an instrumental incorporating very extended soloing as well Indian tonic scales. The album's sleeve

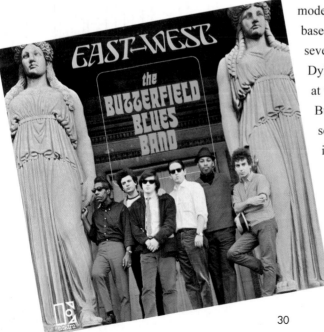

In-flight entertainment
with Frank Zappa

notes even trouble to list the order of the soloists, so the listener immediately knows which of Butterfield's two lead guitarists (Elvin Bishop and Mike Bloomfield respectively) is responsible for which guitar solo. All of this may seem very uncool by today's standards, but there was a moment in the mid-1960s when the approach was fresh, innovative, even radical. The subsequent increasing focus on the lead guitarist's virtuoso role has no direct connection with the concept album. But the stretching of the rock audience's attention-span beyond three or five minutes was initially achieved mainly through instrumental improvisations or semi-improvisations, approached in the same spirit as jazz and generally using a blues-based chord structure as the musical underpinning, over which the lead instruments played their solos.

1966 was a transitional year for the pop industry, when the conventions of recorded pop underwent a preliminary loosening-up process, in preparation for the complete sea-change that hit the industry in 1967-68, in the wake of *Sgt Pepper* and a dozen other ground-breaking albums. The Rolling Stones' 1966 *Aftermath* features the extended blues jam 'Goin' Home', one of the very few long tracks the Stones ever recorded. By the time of Jimi Hendrix's *Electric Ladyland* (1968), the extended 12-bar blues jam had ceased to be a novelty and had instead become an expected album-filling commodity. Even Hendrix struggles to do anything unexpected within the limitations of this formula on 'Voodoo Chile', and the much shorter, heavy rock version of the song, 'Voodoo Chile (slight return)', is more highly regarded. But despite defeating even the most talented rock and blues guitarist of his era, the long ten-minute-plus blues jam remained part of the rock landscape well into the 1970s. Not all 'long' tracks of the late sixties were blues-based, however. Dylan's 'Sad Eyed Lady of the Lowlands' is simply a longer-than-average song, with a regular verse-chorus structure. The Doors' eponymous first album includes the slow-burning 'The End', lyrically-driven but building twice to instrumental guitar/keyboard climaxes that always remain in proportion to the emotion and dynamics of the song as a whole, never tipping over into aimless jamming. Also carefully controlled is The Who's 1966 long track 'A Quick One While He's Away', which sounds much like try-out for the later, more ambitious *Tommy*. Although it clocks in at an impressive nine minutes, the experience of listening to 'A Quick One While He's Away' is more akin to hearing a medley of short songs played in rapid succession. A slight narrative (an extramarital affair is followed by a reconciliation) does not tempt The Who to aim for an ambitious musical structure, or even an attempt at closure via a reprise of the opening theme. Nevertheless, 'A Quick One While He's Away' was a first step en route to the full-blown rock operas *Tommy* (1969) and *Quadrophenia* (1973), as well as the abandoned *Lifehouse* project (concerning a ban on rock and roll in a future dystopian society) that emerged in a modified form as 1971's *Who's Next.*

In contrast, The Mother's Of Invention's first long track, 'Return of the Son of Monster Magnet', from their 1966 debut album *Freak Out,* is a complex creation containing *music concrète,* aleatory vocals, speeded-up tapes and orchestral percussion instruments. Startlingly *avant garde* for 1966, 'Return of the Son of Monster Magnet' and the entire *Freak Out* album anticipates much of Zappa's later work, and, in terms of quality, is the equal of most of his later recorded output. By 1969, tracks long enough to fill one complete side of an album had become a standard feature of the emerging Progressive Rock genre: Iron Butterfly's 1969 'In-A-Gadda-Da-Vida' is a typical example. What is basically a conventionally-structured song (verse-chorus, verse-chorus) which could have been dispensed with in four or five minutes is massively extended via a long, atmospheric and initially very muted instrumental section, dominated by Doug Ingle's 'churchy' organ sound. The instrumental section builds to a powerful crescendo, signalling the re-introduction of the thunderous 'heavy' main theme (this moment was dramatically exploited in the 1986 Michael Mann thriller *Manhunter*). This is a structure similar to Jimi Hendrix's other 1968 long track, '1983 (A Merman I should turn to be)' and its interpolated instrumental 'Moon, turn the tides… gently gently away'.

The licence to expand a musical idea outside any constraints imposed or implied by the single format is a key ingredient in the development of the concept album. The other key ingredients are the readymade models for large-scale composition imported into rock from religious, theatrical and orchestral music: the mass, the musical and the opera. With the sudden expansion of rock's horizons in 1966-68, all of these established forms were used as the basis for rock compositions.

The Electric Prunes' *Mass in F Minor* (1967), a rock version of the Catholic Mass sung in Latin, is probably now best remembered for the 'Kyrie Eleison' section, which is used on the sound track of *Easy Rider* (1969). Out of critical favour for many years, this and the Prunes' follow-up *Release of an Oath* have both been sampled by rap artists in recent years, and so may yet re-emerge as cult classics.

Hair – The American Tribal Love-Rock Musical opened on Broadway on December 1967, and in London the following September. The 1968 Broadway cast, who made the cast album recording, included future Woody Allen foil Dianne Keaton, as well as two of the show's creators, Gerome Ragni and James Rado. The third musical force behind *Hair,* the short-haired, classically-trained composer Galt McDermot, chose not to join the cast and get his kit off. More important as a theatrical and cultural watershed than as a rock album, the theatrical *Hair* and its associated album defined the genre of the rock musical, which rapidly became a big-money genre on Broadway and in the West End, and has come to dominate certain aspects of live theatre. Based on Shakespeare's *Othello*, *Catch My Soul* by Emil Dean and Ray Pohlman, with lyrics by legendary TV producer Jack Good, premiered at London's Roundhouse in 1968. In 1971, Andrew Lloyd-Webber and Tim Rice's *Jesus Christ Superstar* opened in London and the rest, as the saying goes, is history. Rock musicals written for the stage are a curious hybrid, and the influence of the classically-trained McDermot on *Hair* and the academic background of Lloyd-Webber are revealing of the genre's closer relationship to traditional musicals rather than rock. It is in practice very difficult for a heavily-amplified rock sound to alternate on stage effectively with unamplified dialogue scenes: the difference in sound levels is so great. The ensemble all-cast vocal of, say, *Hair*'s opening number 'Aquarius' are a long way from the blues or rock and roll performance tradition: it is arguably closer to a radical updating of the big band sound of the 1940s. Few performers been able to make this hybrid vocal style work away from the particular demands of the theatrical stage.

The third readymade model for large-scale narrative and composition which rock adopted from classical music was the opera. Somewhat ironically, modern classical opera has consistently struggled for audience attention over the last fifty years in competition with the works of the past. An impresario intent on filling Covent Garden or the Paris Opera, will probably choose works by Puccini, Verdi or Wagner over those of John Cage, Cornelius Cardew or Lynne Plowman. Yet opera (according to Wagner the highest art form of all, because it included all the others) continues to act as a kind of magnet which draws pop performers towards its grandeur and perceived cultural status. The Who's *Tommy* was conceived and recorded as a musical behemoth, filling up a total of four LP sides on its release in 1969. The following year, The Who performed Tommy in concert at the New York Metropolitan Opera House – the first rock group to play there. Although Pete Townshend is reported to have been cynical about this penetration of the bastions of high culture, the band nevertheless chose to play the gig.

Tommy is unquestionably a major work, which broadened the potential boundaries of rock music. Nevertheless, *Tommy* is also a giant built on a dwarf's skeleton. The story is even slighter than the plot of most classical operas. Deaf, dumb and blind Tommy is perhaps intended to be a metaphor for adolescence or teenage angst, but as such he has never attracted much analysis from critics or even enthusiasm from fans. Attention has, instead, always tended to be directed towards the individual tracks. Musically, the album unfolds is a series of separate performances. It includes the outstanding 'Pinball Wizard' and several other fine performances such as 'I'm Free', but these are still a series of individual songs without the

The Who's Pete Townshend,
pictured in 1974

musical unity that true operatic writing surely demands - whether essayed in the classical or rock idiom. In truth, one suspects that the public, even The Who's committed fans, have never taken the grandiose pretensions of *Tommy* or the later *Quadrophenia* all that seriously, any more than they took too seriously the pseudo-concept album format of the 1967 album *The Who Sell Out*. Who albums always include a few great tracks, and the band was regarded by many in the late sixties and early seventies as the best live act around. Set against that, the critics, reviewers and fans were prepared to forgive them almost anything. The Who re-recorded *Tommy* in collaboration with The London Symphony Orchestra for the 1975 movie release, a visual extravaganza directed by the inimitable Ken Russell, which belongs more to the history of cinema than to rock music.

Jefferson Airplane's *After Bathing at Baxter's* (1967) was the San Francisco band's deliberately less-commercial follow-up to their hit album *Surrealistic Pillow*, released earlier in the same year. Not exactly a concept album, *Baxter's* is nevertheless held together thematically by its clear intention to embody and disseminate the spirit of San Francisco in 1967: to recreate the Haight Ashberry vibe wherever the album might be played. The album's chaotic non-structure, ostensibly organised into a five-part suite, conveys a disorienting psychedelic experience with greater cumulative power than 'White Rabbit' and the other more accessible songs on *Surrealistic Pillow*.

Less interested than were Jefferson Airplane or The Who in producing work that flattered the youthful *zeitgeist* of late-sixties, the work of Frank Zappa and The Mothers of Invention seems to stand ironically aside from the generation gap. Zappa and his band seem as mocking and contemptuous of their own generation as of the over-the-hill over-thirties. Zappa's *Lumpy Gravy* (1967), a part-orchestral composition recording with both The Mothers of Invention and with Zappa conducting the one-off Abnuceals Emuukha Electric Symphony Orchestra, is a sustained raspberry blown in the general direction of what the 'straight' world were learning to call 'freaks' or 'hippies'. *Lumpy Gravy* arguably includes a little too much of the improvised 'stoned' dialogue about 'White Ugliness', 'Pigs and Ponies' and 'Everything in the universe is just one note', but the satire, though heavy-handed, is smack on target. *We're Only In It For The Money* (1968) is Zappa's first *bona fide* concept album, this time recorded in its entirety with the then-current Mothers of Invention line-up. More accessible than *Lumpy Gravy*, being a collection of individual songs rather than a single long composition, *We're Only In It For The Money* is packaged as a blatant send-up of *Sgt Pepper*, complete with photos of The Mothers in *Pepper*-style poses and in full (but very unconvincing) drag. *We're Only In It For The Money* is partly an attack on the hypocrisy of late-sixties rock stars and their hangers-on. The album's songs lampoon the greed which Zappa perceived as lurking beneath the anti-materialist philosophies espoused in public by so many successful recording artists of the period. In appearing to attack The Beatles, Zappa was in danger of biting the hand that feeds, as The Beatles' patronage had been a key influence in facilitating The Mothers' rise to international fame. But the barbed wit of *We're Only In It For The Money* does not seem to have unduly offended the Fab Four. John Lennon subsequently recorded with Zappa in New York in the seventies. Moreover, the 1968 *White Album* is undoubtedly The Beatles most Zappa-influenced recording, particularly in its clashing together of bizarrely diverse musical (and non-musical) styles and its repeated use of alienation effects that force the listener to acknowledge that they are listening to a recorded work.

Other notable candidates for the title of first full-blown rock concept album include The Pretty Things' *SF Sorrow* and the Small Faces' *Ogden's Nut Gone Flake* (both released 1968). The Pretty Things album traces the life story of its protagonist, Sebastian Sorrow, a life which may or may not end in suicide, and certainly doesn't end happily. The Small Faces bring their mod-honed cockney humour to bear on the world of psychedelia in *Nut Gone*. The sense of humour apparent is one reason why *Nut Gone* stands the test of time and is regularly rediscovered by new generations of critics. 'Lazy Sunday', the hit single that closes the first side, is another reason for the album's continued popularity. *Nut Gone's* narrative concept, which is confined to its second side, concerns the search for the causes of the phases of the moon – thus anticipating The Pink Floyd's 1973 subject matter by five years. Equally 'English' in its terms of reference is The Kinks' 1968 'Village Green Preservation Society', a paradoxical lament for a traditional mythic land of comfortable Englishness which the pop revolution of the 1960s had seemed to render obsolete. This would become a staple theme of many British artists. Banned from touring in the USA, The Kinks continued to pursue their self-consciously insular British agenda in the 1969 release *Arthur or the Decline and Fall of the British Empire* (1969). This album, despite the acuity of Ray Davies' songwriting, seems to mark the beginning of the Kinks' slow commercial decline from their 1965-1968 chart-topping peak. The Kinks rediscovered their commercial touch with 1970's 'Lola', a single positioned at the cutting-edge of early-seventies sexual politics, but hindsight suggests that it was Davies' understandable desire to work on a larger canvas that steered the band into a commercial backwater. Another ambitious concept album of the period, which also touches on the theme of English pop culture's relationship with traditionally English values, was Mark Wirtz's 'A Teenage Opera'. This work was left incomplete in 1968 (though it did yield Keith West 'excerpt' single about 'Grocer Jack'). The album was only finally released in its completed form in 1996.

In complete contrast is White Noise's *An Electric Storm* (1969). This album was the brainchild of producer David Vorhaus and composer Delia Darbyshire (the BBC Radiophonic Workshop genius behind the *Doctor Who* theme). *An Electric Storm* starts out as an accessible example of early synthesiser pop, the first side containing both erotic and humorous interludes and several unusual songs, including the memorable 'Your Hidden Dreams'. Side two, in complete contrast, develops into an electronic celebration of the Black Mass. Not quite qualifying as a full-blown concept album, *An Electric Storm* is nevertheless a seminal work both in its early use of synthesised sounds and in the scale of its musical ambitions, which are sustained through the entire album. Something of a well-kept underground secret, *An Electric Storm* is an album which seems to be unearthed and rediscovered by each new generation.

And then, of course, there were The Moody Blues, who staked a major claim for the first successful concept album with 1967's *Days of Future Passed*. 'Nights in White Satin', the hit single, is known to thousands who have probably never explored the album which it concludes. More adept than most at working with orchestral arrangements (though these are too ethereal or treacly for some tastes), The Moody Blues followed up *Days of Future Passed* with *In*

Concept album pioneers The Pretty Things, pictured in 1969

Search of The Lost Chord (1968) and *To Our Children's Children's Children* (1969). Never as influential as their talent and cult status might have warranted, Moody Blues records succeed through the band's craftsmanship and attention to musical detail. Their weakness, perhaps, is their lack of thematic 'bite': in telling the story of a day in the life of an anonymous everyman, *Days of Future Passed* does not seem to take the artistic risks that are second nature to Dylan, The Beatles, Zappa or even The Who. Nevertheless, The Moody Blues (who once described themselves as 'everyone's third favourite band') created an impressive body of work without succumbing to the kind of self-indulgent excesses that the concept album descended to in the hands of lesser talents.

The history of the concept album post-1969, on a record-by-record basis, would require a whole book to itself. 'Progressive' rock acts became heavily involved: King Crimson's *The Lizard* (1970), for example, contains an obscure narrative thread running through its second side. At the *avant-garde* end of the spectrum, The Third Ear Band released *Elements (Air, Earth, Fire and Water)* in 1970, and provided the music for Roman Polanski's movie *Macbeth* (1971) before the band's untimely implosion. 1971 saw the release of the first Motown concept album: Marvin Gaye's masterpiece *What's Goin' On,* which seems effortlessly to achieve both melodic and lyrical unity via an expanded arrangement in the early-seventies Motown house style. Sly and The Family Stone's *There's A Riot Goin' On* (1971) is not presented with any concept album trappings, but is nevertheless a completely unified recording, taking the listener through an extended musical journey somewhat in the manner of The Beatles' *Revolver.*

1972 saw the scope and range of concept albums widen still further: from Jethro Tull's *Thick as a Brick* to David Bowie's *Ziggy Stardust* and from Emerson Lake & Palmer's *Pictures At An Exhibition* to Alice Cooper's *School's Out.* 1973 saw the release of Mike Oldfield's *Tubular Bells* (though this album's great commercial success came the following year) and Rick Wakeman's *Six Wives of Henry VIII.* Concept albums seemed to be everywhere, but they were not dominating the album charts. The music business was changing, becoming ever more segmented. Singles had become a declining market, appealing mainly to the younger record buyer. The split between rock and pop had become irreparable. Soul music and the Motown sound pursued their own quite separate course. No band now existed with the stature of The Beatles, to draw all the separate strands together. The UK singles charts were now dominated by the likes of T Rex, Gary Glitter, Slade, David Cassidy and The Osmonds, while the album charts were populated by spin-off albums from singles-based acts such as the above, middle-of-the-road artists (Jim Reeves, Andy Williams and so on) and rock acts such as Deep Purple, Led Zeppelin and Yes. It did not seem to be an auspicious time for a band with a hitherto chiefly underground reputation to achieve mainstream success through the release of an ambitious and emotionally downbeat concept album.

Pink Floyd's emergence from the commercial obscurity of the underground was achieved through the lyrical and musical accessibility of *Dark Side of The Moon.* But this success would not have been possible without the six years of concept albums from bands as varied as Alice Cooper and King Crimson. Considered as a concept album, *Dark Side of The Moon* avoids the pitfalls that many gifted artists had fallen into in the previous six years. The album does not employ a pre-existing musical structure as an alibi for its ambitious musical aims. *Dark Side of The Moon* is not a rock opera, or a musical, or a church service, or a soundtrack in search of a movie. It presents itself, lucidly, on its own musical terms, as a collection of songs that are linked both harmonically and by various subtle musical and non-musical devices. It does not achieve closure by a simplistic reiteration of its beginning. *Dark Side of The Moon* ends in a place not envisaged at the beginning, in a new, and deeper form of despair and awareness of mortality.

The genuine product of a decade of continuous development of the 12-inch LP format, *The Dark Side of The Moon* achieves an unobtrusive unity that caused many early listeners to completely overlook the album's overall structure. This may be unfortunate, but it is surely preferable to grandiose claims for the unity and ambition of large-scale works that the material itself cannot sustain. *Dark Side of The Moon* is structured at one level simply to make a good album, along lines not dissimilar to a record such as *Elvis is Back!* Pink Floyd's subtler structural ambitions arise from the seriousness of the album's creative intentions, and the intelligence with which those intentions are fulfilled. *Dark Side of The Moon* signalled both the concept album's coming of age, and the redundancy of the genre as a separate marketing category. Any well-structured album can be treated as a concept album in this sense, whether it is *Revolver* or *Dark Side of The Moon*.

Three years after *Dark Side of The Moon's* release, the punk movement would sweep away most of the overblown pomposity of seventies rock. Despite this, in 1979 Pink Floyd would produce a concept album that more than matched the impact of *Dark Side*. It would come to be regarded as the debased art form's defining statement and final triumph.

TWO

BUILDING THE WALL

he Wall is essentially a synthesis of not one but three different groups bearing the name Pink Floyd. By the time *The Wall* was recorded in 1979, Pink Floyd had grown out of their pioneering space cadet roots, and matured into globally successful progressive rock act. *The Wall* was the next step towards what could be considered the third, and last, significant phase in the group's career – as a performance vehicle for a series of introspective records with unified and introspective lyrics. The first and third phases would each be dominated by a different bandmember, and each phase in the group's life has its fans and apologists. *The Wall* would draw upon the first phase of the group's life as inspiration for its narrative, enjoy the last, lingering benefits of the musicality of the 'mark two' Floyd and represent perhaps the most satisfying expression of the emerging 'mark three' Floyd.

The musical ingredients for the first phase of Pink Floyd began to ferment in the early 1960s, but it wasn't until autumn 1965 that the first successful line-up took shape. Although posters for their earliest appearances advertised them as 'The Tea Set' or 'The Pink Floyd Sound', Syd Barrett, Nick Mason, Roger Waters and Rick Wright preferred 'The Pink Floyd' – a moniker frontman Barrett had conjured by combining the names of his favourite Georgia bluesmen, Pink Anderson and Floyd Counsel.

Roger 'Syd' Barrett was born in 1946, and got to know George Roger Waters (born 1944) when the two were pupils at the Cambridge High School For Boys. The pair remained friends through their teenage years, bonded by their interest in music and the fact that each had lost his father. Waters left Cambridge to study architecture at London's Regent Street Polytechnic. He was already in a blues band with another architecture student, drummer Nick Mason (born in Birmingham in 1945), when he asked Barrett to join in 1964.

By 1966, Barrett's drug-taking experiments had begun. 'As far as I know they might have tried LSD,' recalls the students' landlord and occasional keyboard player Mike Leonard. 'Syd was a bit more inventive and he was in with the chemists, trying any known concoction, unfortunately…'

Keyboard player Richard Wright (born in London in 1945) was probably the most talented musician in the proto-Floyd line-ups, but Barrett's idiosyncratic personality would lend the group its earliest identity. 'With Syd the direction changed,' says Wright. 'It became more improvised around the guitar and keyboards. Roger started playing the bass as a lead instrument, and I started to introduce more of my classical feel.'

'You had a tough cookie in Roger,' says Andrew King, the band's original co-manager. 'If he hadn't been in rock and roll I'm sure he would have been an enormously successful architect. You had Nick, with a wonderful showbiz instinct, and Rick, giving it the basis of

Roger Waters, Syd Barrett, Rick Wright and
Nick Mason – the 1967 line-up of Pink Floyd

the musical skills. And you had a genius in Syd. It was a lucky combination.'

Steered in an increasingly experimental direction by Barrett, The Pink Floyd (as they were still known in 1966) found a select but appreciative audience in London's acid-fuelled underground scene. The band played at the launch party for subversive underground newspaper *International Times* in October 1966, and on 23 December played at the opening night of the legendary UFO club. Black-and-white footage of the band filmed at UFO in January 1967 offers an intriguing glimpse of Barrett's Floyd in full flight – against a background of pulsating lights the seemingly random sounds take form as a psychedelic soundscape emerges from the chaos. Barrett flaps his arms like bird in slow-motion flight, Waters chips in with bizarre sound affects, Wright hunches over his keyboards in intense concentration and Mason rises from his drum stool to bang a gong.

Impressed by a recording of the Barrett original 'Arnold Layne' – produced by UFO co-founder Joe Boyd – EMI signed Pink Floyd with a £5,000 advance in February 1967. Recording of the group's debut album, *The Piper at the Gates of Dawn*, began the following month. The album would be dominated by quirky Barrett compositions such as 'Lucifer Sam' and 'Bike', but it was the lengthy instrumental 'Interstellar Overdrive' (well over nine minutes) that gave the best indication of the group's future direction. One of only two group compositions on the record, the trippy qualities of 'Interstellar Overdrive' belied its origins. One of the inspirations for the track was the version of Bacharach and David's 'My Little Red Book' that opened Love's debut album. The other major influence was even more unlikely – Ron Grainer's shambling theme for the popular television sitcom *Steptoe and Son*. In the hands of Barrett and co, the result was a strikingly original musical journey punctuated with evocative space effects culminating in a stirring reprise of the powerful descending motif. *The Piper at the Gates of Dawn* didn't need either 'Arnold Layne' or its' follow up hit 'See Emily Play' to confirm its status as British psychedelia's quintessential statement.

Towards the end of 1967, the behaviour of the increasingly erratic Barrett led Pink Floyd to curtail an American tour, and a collective feeling grew within the band that the band could no longer function while he remained a member. 'We definitely reached a stage where all of us were getting very depressed just because it was a terrible mistake to go on trying to do it,' said Waters in 1973. '[Syd] had become completely incapable of working in the group.'

Pink Floyd endured a brief and dysfunctional period as a five-piece, with Barrett's childhood friend David Gilmour (born in Cambridge in 1947) joining the group in January 1968 as insurance against the unpredictable and sometimes absent Barrett. Gilmour and Barrett had effectively taught each other to play the guitar during their 'A' level studies,

but Gilmour's technical ability had soon overtaken that of his friend. Gilmour seemed like an obvious fifth member, and soon became a musical sparring partner for the equally talented Wright.

Barrett's departure was formally announced in April. Gilmour assumed sole guitar duties and occasional vocals, but Pink Floyd became effectively leaderless. 'I did spend quite a lot of time – more with friends of Syd's than with the guys in the band – really trying to think of ways of helping him, but the ideas in psychiatry and psychological counselling were rather different to what they are now,' says Gilmour. 'We tended to cling to rather trippy-hippie ideas of what was best for him, which I don't think many people would agree with these days.'

The second incarnation of Pink Floyd had its tentative beginnings in the group's second album, *A Saucerful of Secrets*, which was released in June 1968. The album's centrepiece was the ambitious title track, which clocked in at almost 12 minutes. The song broke new ground, having an evolving structure closer to a three-part suite, and achieving musical closure via a series of key changes and vocal and instrumental development that could not be anticipated from the opening. As early as 1968, and despite being in the process of losing Syd Barrett's creative energy, Pink Floyd had assimilated the most recent developments in rock's new format of the long track, and were ready to push the boundaries of the genre forward on their own behalf. David Gilmour was intrigued to see how his new band tackled its most complex composition to date: 'I remember Nick and Roger drawing out 'A Saucerful of Secrets' as an architectural diagram, in dynamic form rather than in any sort of musical form, with peaks and troughs…. It wasn't music for beauty's sake, or for emotion's sake. It never had a story line. Though for years afterwards we used to get letters from people saying what they thought it meant. Scripts for movies sometimes, too.'

The Waters composition 'Set The Controls For The Heart Of The Sun' was an accomplished piece of trance-like psychedelia, notable for an intriguing lyric about a man raving at a wall. One of *Saucerful*'s other Waters compositions, 'Captain Clegg', was less easy on the ear, but marked the first evidence of its author's preoccupation with the futility of war. It was a theme Waters would return to numerous times in subsequent years, although at this stage in his career he shied away from any specific reference to his father, who had been a casualty of the Battle of Anzio in 1944.

Fragments of Barrett performances remained elsewhere on the album, the most notable being 'Jugband Blues', the haunting farewell that closed the second side. Barrett's subsequent solo albums occasionally flickered into life with moments of fragile beauty, but the lasting impression of both *The Madcap Laughs* (recorded in 1969 and released in 1970) and *Barrett* (1970) is hollow and discomforting.

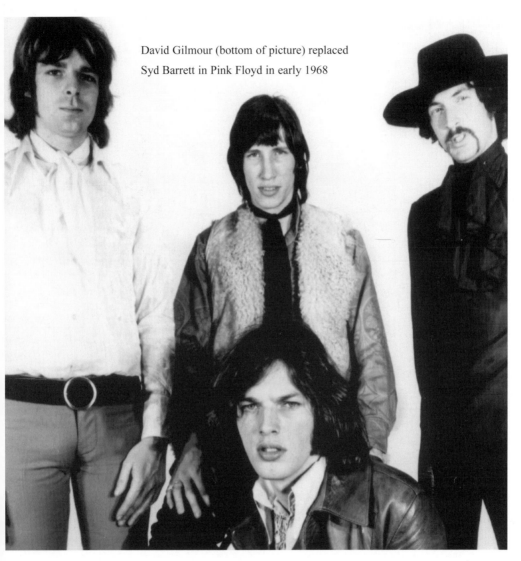

David Gilmour (bottom of picture) replaced
Syd Barrett in Pink Floyd in early 1968

    As Barrett continued his slide into psychosis, the members of his old band floundered in
search of a new musical impetus. Waters started developing ways of expanding the group's
performance beyond the sophisticated light shows they were already famous for. His initial
plans to stage performances inside a circus big top were frustrated (The Rolling Stones'
attempt to film something similar towards the end of 1968 proved almost as problematic
and went unseen for almost 30 years) but he never lost his desire to add a theatrical
dimension to the band's music.

Rick Wright and Roger Waters, pictured
during an early seventies live performance

Nowhere was Pink Floyd's loss of direction more evident than on the band's 1969 double-album *Ummagumma*. Half the album comprised recordings of live performances in Birmingham and Manchester, which included the Barrett-written audience favourite 'Astronomy Dominé'. The second disc was divided into four 'solo' efforts, each composed by a different member of the band. The experiment yielded little material of any interest, but it did require Gilmour to contribute his own compositions, further cementing his position in the group. Waters, in particular, was adamant that that each bandmember should work alone, at one point refusing Gilmour's request that he write some lyrics for his section, 'The Narrow Way'.

The commercial success of the group's next album, *Atom Heart Mother*, was at odds with the half-baked nature of much of its material. Three short compositions, one by Waters, one by Wright and one by Gilmour, were sandwiched between the epic *Atom Heart Mother* suite (at over 23 minutes, occupying all of side one) and the novelty piece 'Alan's Psychedelic Breakfast' (almost 13 minutes). The highlight of this curate's egg was Gilmour's lyrical 'Fat Old Sun', in which his beautiful guitar-playing and gentle vocal effortlessly evoked the Cambridgeshire countryside of his youth. It was perhaps no coincidence that Waters' 'Grantchester Meadows', a track with a more obvious Cambridgeshire reference, had been the standout among the solo elements of *Ummagumma*.

The self-produced *Atom Heart Mother* was released in October 1970 and became Pink Floyd's first number one album. 'At the time we felt *Atom Heart Mother*, like *Ummagumma*, was a step towards something or other,' says Gilmour. 'Now I think they were both just us blundering about in the dark.'

The years may not have been kind to those two albums, but they were valuable steps on the journey that began with 'Interstellar Overdrive' and 'A Saucerful of Secrets'. The group's next album would follow *Atom Heart Mother*'s example by having a side-long track, but would sound altogether more cohesive. The recording of *Meddle* began in January 1971, and although the sessions were initially characterised by failed experimentation the result now stands as the first significant statement by Gilmour/Mason/Waters/Wright line-up, and the most satisfying Floyd album since *The Piper at the Gates of Dawn*. *Meddle*'s reputation is based not on the five songs that comprise side one (although these do include the magnificent instrumental work-out 'One Of These Days'), but the 23-and-a-half minute epic 'Echoes' on side two. The space rock imagery in some of the lyrics recall the group's roots, and are typical of the prevailing progressive rock ethos, but the music and performances heralded the most harmonious era in the group's history. 'Echoes' was the mark two Floyd's most assured musical statement to date.

Meddle would have been an impressive enough achievement for any contemporary band, but history has relegated the album to the status of a forerunner to what is arguably the group's most impressive critical and commercial statement. *Dark Side of the Moon* would build upon 'Echoes', yet forsake the idea of a lengthy track comprising various sections and movements. The tracks on *Dark Side* would segue into each other, creating a cohesive musical feel across *both* sides of the album. Roger Waters assumed responsibility for all the album's lyrics, taking the crucial decision to link the entire piece with a single thematic examination of the causes and effects of madness. The fact that *Dark Side of the Moon* became one of the most successful albums in rock history, bringing the group international success and unimagined wealth, hardly needs repeating. What is perhaps more interesting is that the record on which the reputation of the mark two Floyd rests is rather less than the textbook 'concept album'

David Gilmour and Roger Waters, pictured during studio filming for Adrian Maben's film *Pink Floyd Live At Pompeii* in 1971

it is often held up to be. Scrutiny of the lyrics reveals that *Dark Side* has much more in common with *Sgt Pepper's Lonely Heart's Club Band* than *Tommy*, insofar as that the concept or 'message' is not explicit in every song. Even instrumentals such as 'On The Run' and 'The Great Gig In The Sky' play their part, with Gilmour and Wright willing musical accomplices to Waters' vision.

'We had gelled as a group, we were working very well together and we were working very hard, doing lots of gigs,' says Waters. 'We were in the springtime of Pink Floyd when it was all good fun and we had a common purpose – we wanted to be popular, we all wanted to be rich and famous and we weren't yet… A wonderful time. And it was inevitable that it would all fall apart. Those things tend not to last – and why should they?'

Waters argues that the ultimate message of *Dark Side of the Moon* is one of hope and positivity in the midst of anxiety and despair, but the fact remains that this is the first record that earned him his unwelcome reputation as the gloomiest man in rock. The quality of the music and lyrics are of course contributory factors in *Dark Side*'s astonishing commercial longevity, but it is the lyrics that have transgressed and transcended the changes in musical fashion and taste and which continue to connect with subsequent generations of listeners conditioned to very different styles of popular music. From the irony-bound and cynical 1980s

Nick Mason and
Roger Waters on stage

and beyond, music enthusiasts have generally found more favour with the introspective and melancholy side of 60s and 70s music, and this continuing trend has held *Dark Side of the Moon* in good stead. In an era where Lennon is considered hip and McCartney embarrassing, and in which Nick Drake has risen to prominence while his far more successful contemporary Donovan is now largely overlooked, the introspective and melancholy *Dark Side of the Moon* continues to thrive in numerous repackaged, remixed and remastered editions.

Dark Side of the Moon became the biggest-selling British album of all time (it had sold over 34 million copies by the time of its 30th anniversary re-issue) but its commercial success had an ultimately divisive effect on the band that created it. Having struggled for so long to emerge from the shadow of their absent founder member, Gilmour, Mason, Waters and Wright had now enjoyed unprecedented success.

Ever the strongest motivational force within the group, Waters was determined that the success of *Dark Side* wouldn't rob them of their ambition. He did, nevertheless, realise that the release of the record in March 1973 marked the beginning of the group's disintegration. 'We'd cracked it. We'd won the pools,' he says. 'What are you supposed to do after that? *Dark Side of the Moon* was the last willing collaboration; after that, everything with the band was like drawing teeth; ten years of hanging on to the married name and not having the courage to get divorced; ten years of bloody hell.'

Although this disillusionment was not necessarily a view shared by Waters' fellow bandmembers, when the group reconvened to record the *Wish You Were Here* album in January 1975 the sessions once again felt directionless. Retaining his position as sole lyricist, Waters drew upon what he perceived to be the increased emotional distance between the members of the band when he wrote the lyrics for the album's title track, a mournful elegy for absent friends. The most obvious of all such characters in the band's collective history was of course Syd Barrett, who had long since withdrawn from public view as his psychological problems smothered all trace of his old personality. Syd had been the influence for Waters' lyrics for 'Shine On You Crazy Diamond', the track which, divided into two major sections, opened side one and closed side two. Waters lyrics, which at one point described the subject of the song as a 'piper' and 'prisoner', were set to music of breathtaking beauty by Gilmour and Wright. Gilmour's mournful four-note guitar phrase set the achingly sad tone for the whole piece, which remains one of the most highly regarded songs Pink Floyd ever recorded. Largely on the strength of 'Shine On' and the similarly melancholy title track, *Wish You Were Here* went on to become a worthy critical and commercial successor to *Dark Side of the Moon*.

The recording of *Wish You Were Here* was distinguished by an encounter at Abbey Road Studios that has since passed into legend. During the mixing of 'Shine On You Crazy Diamond' in June, Rick Wright noticed strangely dressed visitor sitting at the back of the studio. The obese stranger had no hair and no eyebrows but, after a short while, began to seem familiar. It was Syd Barrett, returning to offer his services to his old band. 'He was jumping up and down, brushing his teeth,' recalls Wright. 'It was awful. Roger was in tears. It was very shocking. Seven years of no contact, and then to walk in while we were actually doing that particular track. Coincidence? Karma? Fate? Who knows, but it was very, very, very powerful.'

It was widely believed, not least of which by the members of Pink Floyd, that Barrett's psychosis was at least partly triggered by his frequent consumption of such powerful hallucinogens as LSD. But it seems likely that Barrett's withdrawal was also a reaction to the pressures that came with the group's initial success. As the only songwriter of any real consequence, the fate of the group seemed to lie in his hands. This meant that Barrett's commitment effectively extended to EMI, and the pressures of life in a hit-making group were too much to bear.

Coincidentally, *Wish You Were Here* also included a savage attack on record company incompetence in the form of the Waters track 'Have A Cigar'. For Waters, Barrett's brief and sudden reappearance was a disturbing reminder of the possible consequences of life in the music industry's rat race. During the recording of *Wish You Were Here*, Waters was facing personal pressures of his own – the break-up of his marriage. 'Syd's state could be seen as being symbolic of the general state of the group,' he admitted in October 1975, 'ie very fragmented.'

The band spent much of 1976 recording their next album, *Animals*, in their own Britannia Row Studios. The album contained only five songs, and the idea behind Waters' latest concept was easy to fathom from titles such as 'Dogs', 'Sheep' and 'Pigs (Three Different Ones)'. The bleak imagery of the lyrics was matched by a raw and more direct quality to the music; in fact *Animals* was more attuned to the gathering storm of punk than many of the band's detractors were prepared to admit.

Animals was the first Floyd album not to feature any songwriting contributions from Rick Wright, whose attention was being diverted by personal problems such as the imminent break-up of his marriage. 'Roger was changing,' says Wright. 'He really did believe that he was the leader of the band, really did believe that it was only because of him that the band was still going... Recording *Animals* he started rejecting what I came up with. But it was partly my fault, I can see that now, because I didn't push my material. Or I was too lazy to write anything. I suppose he thought, what was the point of having this man in the band?'

Much of the material for *Animals* was honed in live performances prior to the album's release in January 1977, but the band spent the next six months promoting the record on the 'In The Flesh' global tour. The experience proved especially traumatic for Waters, who was feeling increasingly alienated from his bandmembers and his audiences. Pink Floyd's post-*Dark Side* status meant that intimate and even medium-sized venues were now a thing of the past. Previously attentive audiences, who maintained respectful silences during the group's quieter and more intricate songs, had seemingly disappeared. The group's audiences were still highly appreciative, but seemed noisy and raucous in comparison with what had gone before. The bad had been famed for their light shows since the mid sixties, but in more recent years had projected abstract film sequences above their heads, the latest of which featured specially commissioned animation based on designs by cartoonist Gerald Scarfe.

The 'In The Flesh' tour even included giant inflatables, including a pig which hovered over the heads of the audience. The bandmembers were happy to recede in the audience's view, preserving their anonymity behind the lights, films and inflatables. Waters was even further detached, cocooned inside a cumbersome pair of headphones relating a click-track that helped

Roger Waters on stage during the troubled 'In The Flesh' tour of 1977

him stay in synch with the films. This strategy had the unforeseen side effect of eroding the respect certain audience members had for the band, much to Waters' annoyance. When a firework landed on stage during a 3 July performance at Madison Square Garden Waters angrily retorted: 'You stupid motherfucker. And anyone else in here with fireworks, just fuck off and let us get on with it.'

The final night of the tour, three days later, was a watershed in Waters' relationship with his audience. During the performance in front of 80,000 people at Montreal's Olympic Stadium he lashed out at a teenage fan who was clawing his way up the storm netting that separated the audience from the stage. 'Halfway through, I found myself spitting on one particular guy who wouldn't stop yelling,' admitted Waters in 1980. 'He wasn't interested in the show. None of the audience was really responding in any genuine way to what was going on on stage; they were all interested in their own performances. There was a real war going on between the musicians on stage and the audience.'

The gig, and the tour, ended not with the traditional reprise of an audience favourite, but with an improvised blue jam. A disillusioned David Gilmour watched the encore from the mixing desk, unwilling to remain on stage any longer.

Waters was angry and ashamed, and determined that he would never again put himself in such a compromised position. He articulated his concerns to Canadian record producer Bob Ezrin, who had previously been responsible for records by Alice Cooper and Kiss. 'On the *Animals* tour, they stopped in Toronto where I was living,' he remembers. 'On the limousine ride out to the gig Roger told me about his feeling of alienation from the audience and his desire sometimes to put a wall between him and them. I recall saying flippantly, "Well why don't you?"'

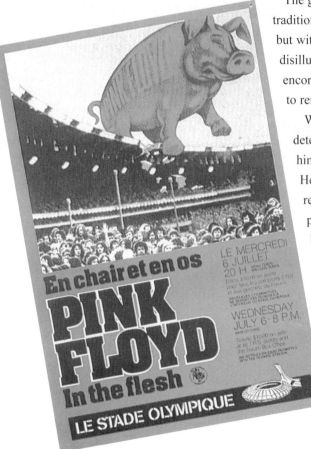

By the time Waters had gathered his ideas back in England, Pink Floyd had entered its third, increasingly fractious phase. Waters would prepare the demos for the next two albums alone – if Pink Floyd had any future at all it would be as a vehicle to articulate his musical ambitions and lyrical preoccupations. But at the end of 1977, there seemed little impetus to continue the group from any quarter.

Nick Mason was the first group member to strike out on his own, as producer of *Music For Pleasure*, the second album by The Damned. The punk pioneers had reportedly asked their record company, Stiff, if Syd Barrett could produce the record. Upon learning that Barrett was unavailable, Mason was offered as a seemingly logical substitute. The album was released in November, and did little to boost the cred of either group or producer with their respective fanbases.

By winter 1977, David Gilmour was working on his first solo album. Keen to capture some of the relaxed spontaneity he felt had been ironed out of Pink Floyd, he recruited drummer Willie Wilson and bassist Rick Wilson, both of whom he had played in bands with in the mid-sixties. The album, titled simply *David Gilmour*, was produced at the Super Bear Studios in France. The two highlights of this unassuming record were 'Short and Sweet', a song Gilmour co-wrote with his friend Roy Harper (who previously handled the vocals on 'Have A Cigar') and 'There's No Way Out Of Here', a cover of a song by the band Unicorn, with whom Gilmour had recently collaborated.

No sooner had Gilmour and co vacated Super Bear than Rick Wright moved in, recording his solo album *Wet Dream* between January and February 1978. Wright's band included guitarist Snowy White, who had joined Pink Floyd on stage during the 'In The Flesh' tour, and saxophonist Mel Collins. Roughly split between vocal tracks and instrumentals, the jazz-influenced *Wet Dream* was even more laid back than *David Gilmour*, and more firmly rooted in the more fluid musical style that Pink Floyd had employed for *Dark Side of the Moon* and *Wish You Were Here*.

While *David Gilmour* made a modest impact on the charts, *Wet Dream* sank without trace, meaning that, in 1978, relatively few Floyd fans could guess at the musical differences which had emerged between Waters on one side and Gilmour and Wright on the other. Such considerations were not at the forefront of Waters' mind when he started to write *The Wall* in autumn 1977. Neither *The Wall* (the realisation of the idea he had outlined to Bob Ezrin) or his other project, another concept album called *The Pros and Cons of Hitchhiking*, were necessarily designed with Pink Floyd in mind. Much of the writing of *The Wall*, in particular, would reach an advanced stage before anyone else in the band contributed.

In the early stages of planning *The Wall*, two images were forefront in Waters' mind. The first was of a wall itself, spanning a stage as a physical embodiment of the barrier between group and audience at such events as the Olympic Stadium concert. The second was a visualisation of what Waters considered to be the sado-masochistic relationship between group and audience. Waters imagined bombing the audience, the 'lucky sections' responding with glee as they received direct hits. 'Those places weren't built for music, they were built for sporting events, and it's not unnatural to experience a ritualisation of war, because that's all sport is,' said Waters of the large venues Pink Floyd had been playing since *Dark Side of the Moon*. 'There is something a bit macabre and worrying about that relationship – that we will provide a PA system so loud that it can damage you and that you will fight to sit right in front of it so you can be damaged as much as possible.'

The idea of actually constructing a wall would be saved for the theatrical presentation of the concept that Waters always believed would follow the album's release. The sado-masochistic element of the concert ritual would survive in the harrowing story Waters devised for *The Wall*. While Waters was quick to point out that *The Wall* was not an autobiographical piece, he conceded that elements of the story were inspired by personal experience. These are easy to identify – the loss of his father at an early age, his unhappy school life, his first-hand experience of Syd Barrett's schizophrenia, his marital break-up and his dislike of stadium shows were all manifested among the more extreme elements of the storyline.

Waters presented demos of *The Wall* and *The Pros and Cons of Hitchhiking* to Gilmour, Mason and Wright in July 1978. The band spent some time working on both, before Gilmour and Mason's concerns about the intensely personal nature of *Pros and Cons* led them to nominate *The Wall* as the next Pink Floyd project. 'It was excruciating to listen to,'

says Gilmour, 'but you could tell instantly that there was a great idea in there.'

Waters had presented *The Wall* to his bandmates in the form of a 90-minute demo which, although of reportedly poor sound quality, featured songs that all agreed held considerable promise. While it was clearly an extension of ideas the band had previously explored in their longform experiments and recent concept albums, the dominance of *The Wall*'s narrative and its rigid operatic feel meant that it was quite unlike anything the band had ever recorded before.

In September 1978, a crisis in Pink Floyd's finance introduced a new urgency to the proceedings. Mismanagement of the band's financial affairs by its collecting agents, the Norton Warburg Group, had lost Pink Floyd a sum that would total £2.5 million. A number of risky investments had failed to bear fruit, and the band was facing a daunting tax liability. The band, and its manager Steve O'Rourke, decided to cut their losses, going on to sue NWG (in June 1987 accountant Andrew Warburg was sentenced to three years in jail for fraudulent trading and false accounting between October 1978 and March 1981).

Pink Floyd's cash flow crisis could be best alleviated with an advance for a new album, and Britannia Row was duly booked for development work which would take up the rest of the year. Rick Wright was disappointed in what he described as the songs' 'fixations' with certain elements of Waters' personal life, but felt there was little alternative but to press ahead with the project.

In the autumn, two months into the group's work on *The Wall*, Waters invited Bob Ezrin to visit him at home and give him his opinion on the demo. Waters' choice of Ezrin may have been motivated in part by other, non-musical factors. 'My job was to be Henry Kissinger – to mediate between two dominant personalities,' said Ezrin in 1993, recalling the way he mediated between Waters and Gilmour. 'Each one has a need to express himself in his own style. And sometimes those styles are very different.'

In order to better share Waters' vision of the sometimes complex-seeming narrative, Ezrin organised the songs and sounds into a specific order within a long document which read like a script for an imaginary film. 'I felt who the central character was and I came to the conclusion that we needed to take it out of the literal first-person and put it in the figurative – resurrecting old Pink to whom they had referred to in the past [in 'Have A Cigar']... It was a whole other way of doing things when you're making music, but it helped to crystallise the work. From that point on we were no longer fishing, we were building to a plan.'

Part of the plan included Ezrin's recommendation that the song 'The Death of Sisco' should be dropped entirely. Gilmour, Mason and Wright raised objections to the song 'When The Tigers Broke Free' arguing that its lyrics – which dealt with the death of Waters' father –

were so personal that they seemed out of place in Ezrin's more figurative revision of the concept. This song was also dropped.

The work conducted at Britannia Row at the end of 1978 was focussed on creating a new, more polished demo of *The Wall*. Waters, Gilmour and Ezrin discarded some of the material, but also added new tracks, notably three songs with music by David Gilmour: 'Young Lust', 'Comfortably Numb' and 'Run Like Hell'.

The revised demo that Waters, Gilmour and Ezrin completed by the end of the year was much closer to the double album that would be recorded in 1979, but distinguished from the familiar Pink Floyd sound by prominent synthesisers and the frequent use of sound affects. In 1974 Waters had expressed the opinion that 'the difference between a sound effect and music is all a load of shit', and many of the sound effects introduced on the Britannia Row demo would blur the boundaries between the two, adding an epic, filmic quality to the piece as a whole.

The Wall would be recorded between April and November 1979, but none of that recording would take place at Britannia Row. Although there were obvious economies involved in using their own studio, the band began the new financial year abroad, seeking exile from the then punitive rates of income tax that threatened to further jeopardise their already fragile finances. Recording commenced at France's Super Bear, a studio already familiar to Gilmour and Wright from their recent solo projects.

The time spent at Super Bear was fast-paced and fruitful, even though Waters reportedly found its mountain altitude a difficult environment for his voice. As a result, he and Ezrin decamped to the Miravel studio in Provence to record the vocals separately, while the rest of the band continued work at Super Bear. The times that Gilmour and Waters spent together could be fraught, as Gilmour recalled in 1987. 'As productive as we were, we could have been making better records if Roger had been willing to back off a little bit, to be more open about other people's input. It wasn't like we were all sitting there leaning on him to look out for us. It was a question of him having forced his way to that position, of him being very tough and having more energy for that sort of fighting.'

'It was all done under that English smiling, left-handed, adversarial stance they take, with smiles on their faces and soft voices,' said Ezrin in 1987. 'But basically they were saying, "I hate you, and I'm going to kill you." The war that existed between those two guys was unbelievable.'

The tension in the studio was not confined to the frequent disagreements within the Waters-Gilmour-Ezrin production triangle. Waters was not the only member of the band to feel a growing dissatisfaction with Rick Wright's input, and while there was a significant amount of goodwill towards Wright it was felt that his position was becoming indefensible. While Mason would drum on almost every track on *The Wall*, Wright's keyboard contributions were supplemented by Waters, Gilmour, Ezrin, orchestrator Michael Kamen and session player Freddie Mandell.

Orchestral sessions for the album took place in New York and, following a holiday in August, the band reconvened for further studio work in Los Angeles. Waters knew that meeting the October delivery date would be difficult, so he asked Wright to start work with Ezrin in Los Angeles a week early. Wright's refusal was the final straw for Waters, who proposed that Wright should complete work on the album and keep his share of its royalties, but then leave the band. Accounts differ over the actual circumstances of Wright's departure – Gilmour maintains he resisted the idea, but Waters claims that both he and Mason endorsed it. He also claims that Gilmour suggested that Mason should go too.

'Roger made it fairly clear that if Rick stayed, he and the album would not,' says Mason. 'I think the threat of what was hanging over us in terms of financial – not just losses but actual bankruptcy – was pretty alarming. We were under a lot of pressure.' Whatever the actual circumstances, the confused Wright was beset by personal problems and had little enthusiasm for *The Wall* anyway. He agreed to go quietly. 'I think in real terms it would be highly likely that I would have been next,' says Mason. 'And then after that I think it would have been Dave.'

Production of *The Wall* finally came to an end in Los Angeles in early November. As the battle-weary Pink Floyd prepared for the most ambitious live shows of their career, Gerald Scarfe put the finishing touches to the double album's gatefold sleeve. *The Wall* was released on 30 November. On oversight on the original print run of the sleeve meant that Rick Wright and Nick Mason received no credit.

Through the means of a non-linear narrative that alternates between the present day, the distant past and nightmarish hallucinations, *The Wall* tells of the painful redemption of a rock star called Pink.

The story begins as Pink recalls a childhood traumatised by the death of his father in the Second World War, an over-protective mother and brutal schoolteachers. Pink's successes in his adult life, and the material possessions they have brought him, cannot compensate for the collapse of his marriage. In the midst of an American tour, Pink suffers a breakdown and descends into catatonia. Locked in his hotel room, Pink is tormented by painful memories of rejection and feelings of worthlessness. A chemical stimulant from an unethical doctor jolts

Pink back into life so he can keep his commitment for that evening's performance. On stage, Pink's paranoia takes hold once again and he hallucinates that he is leading a fascist rally. The audience members become his violent followers, hanging on his every word. Realising things have gone too far, Pink decides to take responsibility for his actions and face the demons from his past. But will he have the courage to tear down the wall he has built to protect himself from the outside world?

Side one of *The Wall* opens with 'In The Flesh?', the title of which makes obvious reference to the *Animals* tour of 1977 while at the same time questioning the validity of the large-scale shows that depressed Waters so much. The Britannia Row demo of this song was entitled 'The Show part 1', and this title still appears on paperwork relating to the Los Angeles sessions, as late as September 1979. Clearly intended to be an extract from of one of Pink's live shows, the pounding drums and buzzing guitars of this bombastic introduction manage to evoke the anger of punk rock and the pomposity of Queen in equal measure.

The Britannia Row demo featured an aggressive-sounding vocal from Waters, which was slightly toned down for the actual recording. The more restrained vocal doesn't stop 'In The Flesh?' making an enormous impact. Although the song doesn't function in the same way as an overture for an opera, its powerful dynamics make it just as arresting. Bob Ezrin recalls creating *The Wall*'s full-bodied presence by recording the basic tracks on a 16-track machine, copying a mixed-down version to a 24-track recorder, taking the drums and bouncing them down to a few tracks and adding them to the 24-track, before adding the overdubs, instruments, sound effects and vocals. His aim was to combine the playback from the 16- and 24-track machines in the hope that the sound from the 16-track machine would be cleaner and brighter because it had been subject to less wear and copying. 'That process has a tremendous amount to do with why that album has got that incredible presence and such a density of sound,' he says.

As Nick Mason's drums splutter to a conclusion the scream of a dive bomber melts into the wails of a baby and David Gilmour sings the opening verse of 'The Thin Ice'. 'It's a flashback, we start telling the story,' explained Waters in 1980, keen to clarify that *The Wall* wasn't strictly autobiographical. 'In terms of this it's about my generation. War-babies. But it could be about anybody who gets left by anybody, if you like.'

The next song, 'Another Brick in the Wall part 1', establishes that the death of Pink's father (killed, it is inferred, during military action) marks the beginning of his neurosis – the first brick in his wall. 'It works on various levels,' said Waters in 1980, keen to emphasise the universal nature of the story's themes. 'It doesn't have to be about the war... I'm the father as well. You know, people who leave their families to go and work, not that I would leave my family to go and work, but lots of people do and have done, so it's not meant to be a simple story about somebody getting killed in the war or growing up and going to school, etc, but about being left, more generally.'

'Another Brick in the Wall part 1' was an additional example of a *Wall* track that sounded more restrained in its ultimate version. The Britannia Row demo included some country-style guitar from Gilmour (an echo of an approach he hadn't favoured since Pink Floyd contributed to the soundtrack of Antonioni's *Zabriskie Point* in 1969) and a piercing scream from Waters, along with some other outlandish vocal effects that were more familiar from his performances in the 1960s.

One of the album's most distinctive sound effects – the noise of a hovering helicopter – heralds 'The Happiest Days of our Lives', the story of Pink's bullying by schoolteachers tortured by their own inadequacies. Waters was prepared to concede that the lyrics of this short song were inspired by his unhappy experiences at the Cambridge High School for Boys. While he had happy memories of his primary school, he recalled that parts of his subsequent schooling were marred by inconsiderate teachers. 'It was awful, it was really terrible,' he said in 1980. 'When I hear people whining on now about bringing back grammar schools it really makes me quite ill to listen to it.'

'The Happiest Days of our Lives' serves as an introduction to the album's best-known song. The Britannia Row demo for 'Another Brick in the Wall part 2' was recorded under the working title 'Education', and resembled a brief guitar and synthesiser jam with Waters' single verse and chorus delivered in the style of a whispered threat. This quietly sinister fragment of a song had more in common with 'Another Brick in the Wall part 1' insofar as it was a bridge between more significant tracks (the demo's droning synthesiser led into the standout 'Mother', which closed side one).

'Another Brick in the Wall part 2' might have stayed that way had Bob Ezrin not decided to experiment with a disco music. He sent Gilmour out to clubs to listen to the style (his verdict: 'Gawd awful!') and then asked Mason to add a disco beat. When he then asked for an additional verse and chorus to extend the track beyond its 1 minute 20 seconds length he received a frosty response, and a reminder that Pink Floyd didn't do singles. When they left, Ezrin started experimenting with his 16- and 24-track set-up, which he used to copy the first verse and chorus. He connected the repeated verse and chorus with a drum fill and then extended the chorus. This still left Ezrin with the problem of the second verse, which couldn't just be a repeat of the first. He drew upon his experience of producing Alice Cooper's 1972 single 'School's Out', and asked one of the album's engineers, Nick Griffiths, to record a group of schoolchildren to sing a repeat of the first verse. Griffiths recruited 23 children, all aged between 13 and 15, from London's Islington Green School, which was near Britannia Row. The tabloid press would later use the incident as a stick to beat the group with, pointing out that the school had a shocking academic record, and that the children hadn't even received a free copy of the album, let alone any payment. The school had, it transpired, been recompensed with free use of the recording facilities at Britannia Row, and the children were hastily provided with complimentary copies of *The Wall*.

Ezrin has fond memories of the moment he presented his 'remix' to the song's author: 'I called Roger into the room, and when the kids came in on the second verse there was a total softening of his face and you just knew that he knew it was going to be an important record.'

'Another Brick in the Wall part 2' became Pink Floyd's first British single since they gave up trying to score hit records with the ill-fated 'Point Me At The Sky' in December 1968. 'Another Brick in the Wall part 2' would fare rather better – following its release ahead of *The Wall* on 16 November it would sell over a million copies, becoming the last number one single of the 1970s and a prescient anthem for those who felt subjugated by the Thatcher government.

'Mother', the last song on side one, was a disturbing description of an over-protective parent restricting her son throughout his childhood years. The character in the song bore no resemblance to Waters' own mother, as he was careful to tell her following the record's release. Waters continues to deny that this part of the record was in any way autobiographical, but the point was reinforced on side four when, during 'The Trial', Waters voiced the character of Pink's mother with a pronounced Yorkshire accent.

'Generally Nick worked hard and played well on *The Wall*,' said Gilmour in 1994. 'He even worked out a way of reading music for the drums. But there was one track called 'Mother' which [he] really didn't get. So I hired Jeff Porcaro to do it. And Roger latched on to this idea, the way he always did with my ideas, and began to think, is Nick really necessary?'

Side two begins with another flashback to the Second World War with 'Goodbye Blue Sky', a song distinguished by the smooth multi-tracked vocals from Gilmour. The next song on the album was originally intended to be 'What Shall We Do Now?', Pink's lament for his inability to compensate for his emotional problems with expensive luxuries and other distractions. It was only when consideration was given to the running time of each side of the LP in autumn 1979 that it was discovered that side two was too long. 'What Shall We Do Now?' was dropped from the album altogether, although it was already too late to revise the inner bag of the first record, which contained the lyrics for the song in their previous position, after

'Goodbye Blue Sky'. 'We didn't go into a great panic about trying to change all the inner bags. I think it's important that [the lyrics] are there so that people can read them,' said Waters in 1980, justifying the decision by saying he felt that reading the words for the lost song would help listeners make the transition from the 'Goodbye Blue Sky' flashback to the present-day events that followed.

'What Shall We Do Now?' was replaced in the final order by 'Empty Spaces', which fulfilled a similar lyrical function. The song is now best known for its backwards message which can be faintly heard around halfway into the song. Enterprising audiophiles risked the styluses of their turntables to decipher the noise as: 'Congratulations. You have just discovered the secret message. Please send your answer to Old Pink, care of The Funny Farm, Chalfont.' Fans of the group suspected that the message was a reference to Syd Barrett, but no official explanation was forthcoming.

The next track, 'Young Lust', was the first on the album to be co-written by Gilmour. The track went through three distinct stages of development, making its first appearance as an instrumental on the Britannia Row demo. The funky electric piano and disco-style drumbeat resembled the Bee Gees' 1975 hit 'Jive Talkin'' but, when the first set of lyrics arrived the song started to sound more like a broad pastiche of Status Quo-style hard rock. The second version of the song was the first to feature lyrics, the first draft of which Waters recalled were about a young school-leaver 'hanging around outside porno movies and dirty bookshops', feeling a compulsion about sex but being too inhibited to do anything about it. The finished version of the song, which included knowingly clichéd references to a 'dirty woman' and a 'rock and roll refugee', featured a roared vocal from Gilmour which reminded Waters of his performance on the 1969 track 'The Nile Song'.

The AT&T telephone operator that appeared at the end of 'Young Lust', trying to connect a transatlantic call from 'Mr Floyd' to the unfaithful 'Mrs Floyd', was apparently unaware that she was part of *The Wall*'s narrative. Her confusion at her repeated failure to put the call through was genuine, and Waters was delighted by her performance.

From this point on it becomes clear that the story has shifted to Pink's hotel room in America. Clearly disillusioned with his adulterous and uncommunicative wife, he invites a groupie into his room. The groupie admires his collection of guitars and his generously sized bath tub, before Pink goes crazy and starts to smash up the room. The Britannia Row demo of 'One Of My Turns' featured a more extensive monologue by the groupie and a thin-sounding synthesiser accompaniment to Waters' hysterical vocal. The groupie's compliments over Pink's guitars and the quality of his hotel room stand in clear contract to the sense of emptiness that is engulfing him. At the time of *The Wall*'s release, Waters admitted that the lyrics of 'One Of My Turns' had been indicative of his once cynical attitude towards marriage, but pointed out that the song was by no means autobiographical.

'One Of My Turns' is followed by 'Don't Leave Me Now', in which Pink is forced to accept the end of his marriage, and 'Another Brick In The Wall part 3', although the inner bag of the original vinyl release had 'Empty Spaces' in this position on the record. The final track on side two is 'Goodbye Cruel World', which represents a final message from Pink before he slips into catatonia.

The running order on side three of *The Wall* was subject to the same debate and last-minute amendment as side two. The album's second disc was supposed to open with 'Is There Anybody Out There?' (essentially the same line repeated over and over again) and the LP's inner bag reflected this accordingly. When Ezrin called Waters to air his concerns over side three, Waters responded with a radical solution. He proposed that 'Hey You' could fit anywhere in the record's narrative, and suggested that the best place for it would actually be at the beginning of this side. 'The reason that all these decisions were made so late was because we'd promised lots of people a long time ago that we would finish this record by the beginning of November, and we wanted to keep that promise,' he recalled in 1980.

'Hey You' features the first reference to worms, which in this song are described as eating into Pink's brain. There would be further references to worms on side four, but the original draft of Waters' lyrics had contained a much greater use of the image as a symbol of the decay brought on by isolation.

In the final running order, 'Hey You' is followed by 'Is There Anybody Out There?' and 'Nobody Home', the last song to be written for the album. 'Nobody Home' is probably the most haunting track on *The Wall*, and takes the listener back to the late sixties with references to the then fashionable Gohills boots, Jimi Hendrix perms and satin shirts. 'There are some lines in here that hark back to the halcyon days of Syd Barrett,' said Waters in 1980. 'It's partly about all kinds of people I've known, but Syd was the only person I used to know who used elastic bands to keep his boots together, which is where that line comes from.'

The next song, 'Vera', is a lament for the forces' sweetheart who sang 'We'll Meet Again'. Its appearance in the narrative is prompted by the film *Battle of Britain* appearing on Pink's television set. The demo version of the song featured croaking vocals from Waters, whose performance was rather more listenable on the finished record.

The sound of military drums links 'Vera' to 'Bring The Boys Back Home'. Gilmour regards this to be one of the weakest sections of the album, but Waters considers it to be absolutely central. In 1980 he explained why: 'It's partly about not letting people go off and be killed in wars, but it's also partly about not allowing rock and roll, or making cars, or selling soap, or getting involved in biological research or anything that anybody might do, not letting *that* become such an important and 'jolly boys' game' that it becomes more important than friends, wives, children, other people.'

On the Britannia Row demo the song was followed by parts 2 and 3 of 'Is There Anybody Out There?', neither of which made it onto the album, and a track that studio paperwork listed as 'The Doctor'. The lyrics of the demo version are very different from those of the song as it ultimately appeared, but they tell the same story – Pink is found in his hotel room and an unscrupulous doctor gives him enough stimulants to jolt him out of his catatonia. He is taken, in a drugged and confused state, to the next show of his American tour.

'The Doctor' is a fascinating work-in-progress glimpse into the construction of what became one of Pink Floyd's best-loved songs – 'Comfortably Numb'. 'Things like 'Comfortably Numb' are really the last embers of Roger and my ability to work collaboratively together – my music, his words,' says Gilmour. The track started life as an instrumental demo based on an out-take from the *David Gilmour* sessions. 'I fought for the introduction of the orchestra on that record – the expansion of the Floyd's sound to something that was more orchestral, theatrical… 'filmic' is the word,' said Ezrin in 1993. 'This became a big issue on 'Comfortably Numb', which Dave saw as a more bare-bones track, with just bass, drums and guitar. Roger sided with me. So 'Comfortably Numb' is a true collaboration – it's David's music, Roger's lyric and my orchestral chart.'

The lyrics that feature on the Britannia Row demo are notable for the way Waters rhymes 'listen', 'physician', 'condition' and 'magician', recalling the child-like wordplay of Syd Barrett on early Pink Floyd tracks such as 'Bike'. Despite these differing lyrics, the duet between him and Gilmour – which Gilmour has subsequently described as him representing the light side and Waters representing the dark – is clearly worked out, with Waters' spoken section resembling Bob Dylan in places.

Both versions of the lyrics were based on Water's own experience, as he explained in 1980: 'I had one [doctor] once who thought I'd got food poisoning or an upset stomach. He told me I had a viral infection of the stomach or something, and he thought I had stomach cramps. He wasn't listening to me at all, I don't think. In fact, I discovered later that I had hepatitis. He gave me three tranquilisers; we were in Philadelphia, and boy, those were the longest two hours of my life, trying to do a show when you could hardly move your arm… I thought, if he'd have just left me alone, the pain I could have coped with – that was no sweat – but I could hardly lift my arms, or any of my limbs…'

The guitar solo that ends 'Comfortably Numb', and side three of *The Wall*, sounded too 'clean' for Gilmour's liking, but he was outvoted when he tried to change it. The expanded version of 'Comfortably Numb' that has been performed live by Pink Floyd since 1987 has always included a grungier guitar sound of the type Gilmour would have preferred to have included on the record.

Side four of *The Wall* takes the narrative out of Pink's wrecked hotel room and into the concert hall for his next performance. The first track, 'The Show Must Go On', leads to a reprise of 'In The Flesh' (now minus its question mark) as Pink begins his next gig. The bombastic music is the same, but Pink is clearly a changed man – he tells the audience that illness forced Pink to stay behind, explaining that he is now fronting a 'surrogate band'. Pink behaves like a fascist, turning the spotlight onto the ethnic minorities and other 'undesirables' in the audience. In 1980 Waters was quick to stress that 'In The Flesh' was supposed to be obnoxious, careful to preclude any accusations that Pink's delusions were in any way representative of his own political beliefs.

The next song performed by the deluded Pink and his surrogate band was Waters' final collaboration with Gilmour. 'Run Like Hell' was based on another out-take from *David Gilmour*, and first appeared as an instrumental on the Britannia Row demo. The demo would have sounded very similar to the finished article were it not for the absence of Rick Wright's distinctive synthesiser. Gilmour's resonating guitar riffs are obvious successors to his work in the closing minutes of 'Sheep' from *Animals*, and helped make 'Run Like Hell' one of the most powerful tracks on the album. An extended version of the song would become a traditional encore performance at Pink Floyd concerts during the 1980s and 90s.

The harmonised vocals that open the next song, 'Waiting For The Worms', make it sound one of the more dated tracks on the album, firmly identifying its late seventies origins. The demo version of the song ended with a plane crash, but on the album Pink's fascist rant is drowned out by the crowd chanting 'Hammer, hammer…', the significance of which wouldn't become clear until the live performances. The crescendo is curtailed by 'Stop', the song in which Pink can finally bear no more and prepares to make himself accountable for his actions.

'Stop' leads into 'The Trial', an outrageous piece of musical theatre co-written by Waters and Ezrin. The song, which was demo'd under the title 'Trial By Puppets', has Waters voicing the schoolmaster, Pink's wife, Pink's mother, Pink himself and the judge in what must surely be the most bizarre song on this or any other Pink Floyd album.

On 'Trial By Puppets', an almost jaunty piano performance (probably by Ezrin) made

Artist Gerald Scarfe, pictured in 1990 with one of the animation cels he designed for the film *Pink Floyd The Wall*

an eerie accompaniment to Waters' theatrical vocals. On both versions of the song, Gilmour reprises the strident riff from 'Another Brick in the Wall part 2' before Pink – who is of course judge, prosecutor and defendant – sentences himself to tear down his own wall.

The wall explodes, leading to the final track, 'Outside The Wall'. 'At the end of it all... his judgement on himself is to de-isolate himself, which in fact is a very good thing,' said Waters in 1980, explaining what he considered to be the album's essentially positive message. There is a twist in the tale, however – during the closing seconds of side four, an almost inaudible Waters can be heard saying, 'Isn't this where...'. The opening seconds of side one feature a similarly quiet Waters saying, '...we came in.' The suggestion being that the destruction of personal walls is something that we must strive to do over and over again if we are to avoid the 'worms'...

The Wall had cost an estimated $700,000 to record, but if there were any fears about this expenditure they were soon allayed. The album shipped over a million copies in its first eight weeks, displacing The Bee Gees' *Greatest Hits* at the top of the US album chart. It stayed there for 15 weeks.

Elements of the post-punk music press were predictably scathing about the record, but elsewhere there was a more constructive debate over its merits, and especially its standing in relation to *Dark Side of the Moon*. Waters' thoughts had already turned to the elaborate theatrical presentation of *The Wall*, which he had always considered a crucial facet of the piece.

Planning for the stage presentations had in fact begun before the formal studio sessions for the album even commenced. Mark Fisher and Jonathan Park, design and engineering experts respectively, had previously worked with Pink Floyd on the 'In The Flesh' tour, and were recalled to help Waters realise his ambitious aspirations for *The Wall*. Fisher began sketching his first stage designs in January 1978, but had to wait until September before he received the formal go-ahead. During the mixing and sequencing sessions in France the band had created a mock-up of the concert stage on a table-top, and populated their miniature theatre with plastic figuures and models representing the inflatables in an effort to visualise the elaborate stage show.

Aside from Fisher and Park, Waters' other new collaborator for *The Wall* shows was art director Gerald Scarfe, whose grotesque drawings of such major characters as Pink's mother and wife, the schoolmaster and the judge – as well as rows of goose-stepping hammers – would feature in animated films created especially for the show. The mother, wife and schoolmaster would be brought to life as giant-sized inflatables, dangled like twisted marionettes over the stage. The animated films would cost around £500,000, and take well over a year to produce.

'The most difficult character to express was Pink himself,' said Scarfe in 1980. 'As I saw him, Pink was the vulnerable spirit in us all; inside the wall and hurt continually by the things that happen in his life. In Roger's piece, the mother hurts him, the teacher hurts him, the wife hurts him… and each one causes a brick or many bricks in the wall to be built up. So I had to start from Pink and eventually, as you know, he ended up as a helpless little pink dummy – almost like the nerve centre or a bare prawn. When you've taken the shell off a prawn, it's vulnerable inside, it's helpless – so I think that he symbolises what's in us all in that way.'

The other characters Scarfe designed were rather less likeable. The mother was an overweight battle-axe wearing austere 1940s-style clothes. Her inviting arms transformed into a rigid embrace as the flesh transformed to brick walls. Scarfe designed Pink's wife as a mantis-like harpie with (literally) flaming hair, and drew upon his own memories of school in creating a spindly teacher with a leering gaze and Hitler moustache. The first sequence Scarfe animated was 'The Trial', which featured a judge who could best be described as a pair of huge stamping buttocks, thereby proving of course that the law really is an ass. Scarfe next embarked on an abstract of twisting, copulating flowers for 'Empty Spaces', which in the live shows segued into 'What Shall We Do Now'. 'What I tried to show in the animation is that one of the walls which we all suffer is the wall of materialism,' said Scarfe in 1980. 'The fact that we hide our pain behind a wall of goods. If you are really harassed, you can buy a new washing machine, a new TV, a new camera or watch or something; a new Ferrari…. A new Lear Jet in some cases… It's not a wall about the real values in life. One builds up this huge wall of consumer goods and that changes everybody, turns them into monsters. At the end of my animation, the character is turned into a hammer.'

The sequences were sometimes highly moving, as in 'Goodbye Blue Sky' for which Scarfe created pathetic, cowering creatures called 'the frightened ones'. Scarfe's work was more generally characterised by a profoundly disturbing feel, and informed by a prevailing anti-Disney ethic. Waters was delighted with his work.

Although Gilmour would be credited as musical director in the shows' souvenir programmes, Waters became increasingly isolated from the other members of Pink Floyd during 1980. The irony wasn't lost on Mark Fisher, who recognised that although *The Wall* was a story about the consequences of non-communication, it had been created by a group who were no longer talking to one another.

At various stages Waters had toyed with the idea of performing the entire show from behind a wall, and continuing construction of the wall throughout the show until it was complete at the end. It was eventually decided to construct the wall during the first half of the show, with the final brick put into position at the end of 'Goodbye Cruel World'. The wall itself comprised 340 cardboard 'bricks' which, slotted together, stretched 160 feet long and 35 feet high. The bricks were carefully weighed to ensure that they wouldn't harm any audience members should they stray from the stage when the wall was demolished at the end of 'The Trial'. While the band remained behind the wall for much of the second half, the completed wall served as an excellent screen on which to project Scarfe's 35mm film sequences, thereby providing the audience with something to look at while they waited for Pink's redemption.

It was relatively late in the planning stages when it was decided to liven up the second act further by installing a section in the structure which would be revealed during 'Nobody Home'. The hole in the wall was dressed as Pink's hotel room, complete with television set and standard lamp, and Waters performed the song while reclining in a chair. The other bandmember to make a surprise appearance during the second half was Gilmour, who performed his searing solo for 'Comfortably Numb' standing on top of a special structure that, to audience members, made it appear that he was standing on top of the wall. Spotlights placed behind him would cast his giant shadow across each auditorium as he played.

The Wall shows would require 45 tons of equipment, and Waters knew that finding suitably sized venues to accommodate them would be difficult. It was originally intended to stage the shows inside a specially designed touring venue. The inflatable tent, a possible throwback to Waters' big top idea from the late sixties, would have been 354 feet long and 82 feet high, with the capacity to seat 5,000. The surviving production drawings show that it resembled a giant blue slug.

It was decided to find a more practical solution, although Waters remained understandably adamant that the shows would not be performed in oversized venues – even when a Philadelphia promoter guaranteed the band a million dollars plus expenses per night for a two-night stint at the JFK Stadium. This self-imposed restriction, and the complexities of the production, meant that *The Wall* would be performed just 29 times over 1980 and 1981.

The touring band comprised Gilmour, Mason, Waters and Wright, with a 'surrogate band' that included Andy Bown on bass, Willie Wilson on drums, Snowy White on guitar and Peter Wood on keyboards. The sound mixing was the responsibility of James Guthrie, who had played a crucial role in the recording of *The Wall* as its engineer and co-producer. 'The main logistical problem of the show was timing,' he says. 'There was just too much to co-ordinate: the inflatable puppets to appear on cue; sound effects; the aeroplane [that crashes at the end of 'In The Flesh?']; Gerald's films etc. Not to mention the building of the wall itself. It was enormously complex.'

There were two months of rehearsals, most of which were conducted for the benefit of the stage-hands who had to quickly assemble the wall and safely demolish it each night, but the band never got the chance to perform a complete run-through without breaks before the opening concert. At the first performance of the show, at the Los Angeles Sports Arena on 7 February 1980, something went wrong. The 16,000-strong audience were impressed by the pyrotechnics that accompanied the close of 'In The Flesh?' unaware that they weren't entirely planned. A stray firework ignited a drape, sending fragments of burning material down on to the stage. When he became aware of the seriousness of the situation Waters stopped the show, only restarting once the fire brigade had quenched the flames. The pyrotechnics were dropped from subsequent performances.

Aside from these teething problems, the Los Angeles shows set the style for the rest of the tour. There were a number of surprises for audiences – the band only played *The Wall*, and no tracks from any other Pink Floyd albums, adding the previously unheard 'What Shall We Do Now?' and a seemingly improvised instrumental prior to 'Goodbye Cruel World'. This song was added in order to synchronise the show so that the final note of 'Goodbye Cruel World' would always coincide with the placement of the final brick. The instrumental on the belated live album *Is There Anybody Out There?*, released in 2000, was given the appropriate title 'The Last Few Bricks'.

During the final Los Angeles show, which took place on 13 February, Waters' old antipathy towards his audience returned. 'In the first half, some asshole was shining a battery-operated pocket laser on the screen,' he complained the day after. 'I didn't do anything because there was so little of that kind of mischief going on; I just thought they'll find him and take his little toy away and break it. It's such a drag for 10,000 people if one person is screwing it up

Gilmour and Waters share vocals during a live performance of *The Wall* in 1981

by having his piece of fun… If they can't understand what I'm trying to do… to fiddle with toys while I'm doing serious work, they should stay at home.'

The tour's next stop was five nights at the Nassau Veterans' Memorial Coliseum in New York, where over 33,000 tickets were sold in just five hours. One of those tickets was bought by Bob Ezrin, who had been banned from the backstage area when he broke Waters' strict secrecy rules by telling a journalist friend about the shows. Leaving aside any hard feelings, Ezrin was overwhelmed by the whole production. When Gilmour performed the guitar solo from 'Comfortably Numb' at the top of the wall he burst into tears.

The shows performed in New York from 24-28 February were a great success, but it was nevertheless estimated that for each night Pink Floyd played *The Wall* Gilmour, Mason and Waters each lost $15,000. Ironically, Rick Wright was immune to these losses – his departure from the band meant that he collected a session player's salary regardless.

'Probably because they were unique at the time, the shows have acquired a couple of myths,' says Mark Fisher. 'One is that they were inordinately expensive to mount, the other that they were nigh on impossible to tour. There's no doubt that they were expensive and that they were a pig to move around… but once everything was in place that was it for a week because the Floyd were able to sell out in any arena for any number of nights. Obviously, that goes a long way to ameliorate the initial costs, as well as the logistics of shifting equipment.'

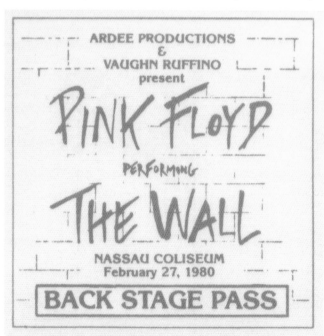

In March 1980, *Melody Maker* reported that Pink Floyd were shifting their equipment to the UK. The article claimed that the band had tentatively booked nine nights at Wembley Arena (formerly known as the Empire Pool) in early June, but had decided instead to play at the larger Earls Court Exhibition Centre. The report also claimed that the band was considering staging the show at an open-air arena in Milton Keynes with a capacity of 35,000. This was probably too close to a stadium environment to please Waters, and the Milton Keynes dates never materialised.

Pink Floyd performed *The Wall* at Earls Court from 4-8 August. Sections from these shows were later included on the *Is There Anybody Out There?* album, including the introduction by the master of ceremonies Gary Yudman, who cautioned the audience against the use of fireworks.

The tour recommenced at the Westfalenhalle in Dortmund, West Germany, from 13-18 February 1981. The final dates were played at Earls Court from 13-17 June later that year. These five performances were mounted specifically to allow Gerald Scarfe and cinematographer Michael Seresin film the shows in their capacity as co-directors of a planned movie based on *The Wall*. 'The shooting was a total disaster,' recalled Alan Parker, who at this stage was acting as the project's producer. 'Michael and Gerry didn't quite gel as directors and I myself, quite useless as an impotent director masquerading as a not-too-helpful producer, began chain-smoking for the first time in my life. From the start, the

dilemma was always compromising the theatrics of the show for the needs of the film… The fast Panavision lenses, needed for the low light levels, had no resolution, so the rushes looked like they'd been shot through soup. A Louma crane shot that scaled the wall to reveal the thousands in the crowd as Roger sang 'Hey You' never got its complicated moves right – and with five live shows it only had five chances, all muffed.'

There was further anguish for Scarfe when, in the early hours of the morning following the final performance ten original pieces of his artwork were stolen from an exhibition that had been held in the foyer. Insurers valued the missing paintings, which included Scarfe's original artwork for the album cover, at £30,000.

For the three members of Pink Floyd and their estranged keyboard player, the end of the *Wall* tour brought a respite from the strained atmosphere that had continued to grow since the recording sessions. Waters recalls with some amusement that

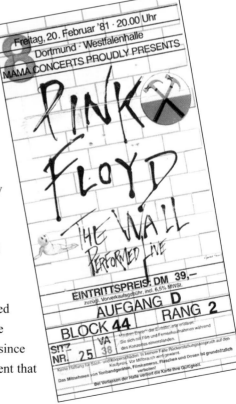

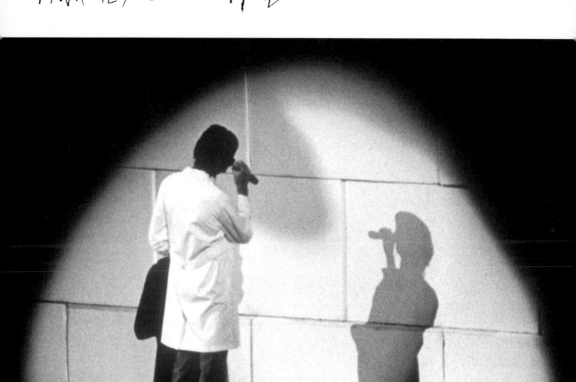

Waters as the unscrupulous doctor during a performance of 'Comfortably Numb' at Earl's Court

before and after the performances each band-member would retire to his own trailer, all of which were arranged so that the doors faced outwards, meaning that nobody had a view of anyone else.

Despite the tensions, each member of the band has fond memories of the brief tour. Even Rick Wright found much to enjoy during his borrowed time. 'I loved the idea of the [surrogate] band appearing in masks and not being us,' he says. 'You go to see a show, you think, Oh there's Pink Floyd on stage, there's Dave, there's Rick, there's Roger. Then a curtain opens and there's another Pink Floyd behind them. I think it was a very good concept once [Roger] had decided to make the wall a feature of the show rather than just a statement to the

A full capacity audience at Earl's Court

audience… On the other hand, it wasn't much fun to play because we were hidden half the time. While you were playing, you had lots of roadies running around, putting things up, taking things down. Very impersonal.'

Wright had been determined to play *The Wall* shows 'as a kind of final goodbye', and they marked the last occasion the Gilmour/Mason/Waters/Wright line-up played together. 'I'm not sure how I did it,' says Wright now. 'I must have completely blanked out my anger and hurt. It was an awkward situation for all of us to be in, but in the English 'stiff upper lip' manner we just got on with the job.'

Ironically, the concert on 17 June would actually prove to be Roger Waters' 'final goodbye'.

He would continue as a member of Pink Floyd until 1985, but would never perform a live concert with the band again. In the absence of any kind of announcement, it would be several years before most fans realised that Wright had left Pink Floyd. By this time, Waters' plans for the group were driving a wedge between him and Gilmour and Mason.

Reflecting on Pink's liberation at the end of *The Wall*, Gilmour draws a parallel with the

character's creator. 'Maybe Roger's statement at the time should have been to leave the band, because that would have been one of *his* catharses.'

But before the final reckoning, Waters embarked on the feature film that he felt would be the ultimate expression of *The Wall*. Of all the different realisations of his story, he would find this the most traumatic and dissatisfying.

THREE

THE WALL

ON SCREEN

The film version of *Pink Floyd The Wall* was prompted by the animated sequences Gerald Scarfe designed for the stage shows, but Roger Waters soon came to regard it as a natural extension of his concept. Unlike the previous incarnations of *The Wall*, however, the movie would take its creator into uncharted territory.

Pink Floyd had been heard – and occasionally seen – in several feature-length documentaries, including *Tonite Let's All Make Love in London* (1967). Produced, written, directed, photographed and edited by Peter Whitehead, this look at swinging London featured interviews with Mick Jagger, Julie Christie, Michael Caine, Lee Marvin, Eric Burden, Vanessa Redgrave and David Hockney. Whitehead also filmed the band recording songs for *Tonite* in *Pink Floyd London '66 – '67* (1967), a 30 minute short. Pink Floyd also featured on *San Francisco (A Day in the Life Of)* (1968), directed by Anthony Stern, and *The Committee* (1968). *San Francisco* included a live performance of 'Interstellar Overdrive'.

Pink Floyd soon caught the attention of German director Barbet Schroeder, who recruited the band for *More* (1969), a drama of young love destroyed by heroin addiction. The director felt Pink Floyd had the right sound for his film: spaced-out and in tune with nature. Music aside, this French-German-Luxemburg co-production is mainly notable for the Paris and Ibiza locations. The dramatic highpoint features American lead Mimsy Farmer injecting drugs under her tongue.

The Pink Floyd tracks composed for *More* included 'The Nile Song', which Waters would later compare to *The Wall*'s 'Young Lust'. According to David Gilmour, the entire soundtrack was written, recorded and edited in eight days. When Barbet Schroeder dropped in at the studio, he was struck by how hard the band worked. Schroeder regarded the finished recording as a total success, requiring no changes. Schroeder didn't use Pink Floyd's songs as a conventional score; the music always had a source within the film, playing on radios and tape machines. At one point, a song abruptly stops as the tape is turned off. Schroeder wanted music his characters were actually listening to, rather than straightforward dramatic underscoring.

More opened in New York City on 4 August 1969, earning some positive reviews. The *New York Times* praised *More* as 'a very beautiful, very romantic movie'. The sex scenes and frequent drug use earned the film an 'X' rating, which hurt its box-office chances. Barbet Schroeder attributed the disappointing US returns to the language barrier. While much of *More* was in English, the script lacked the hippie slang favoured by the American youth culture. According to Schroeder, *More* did much better in Europe, though the British censor demanded cuts – toning down the drug scenes – before granting an 'X' certificate in 1970. On the whole, Schroeder felt he'd made a film that accurately reflected the times. Schroeder also credits

More for introducing Pink Floyd's music to European audiences. That said, the director admitted the film owed much of its fame to the score. After years in semi-obscurity, *More* resurfaced on video in the United States and DVD in France. In Britain, the British Film Institute reissued *More* on video in 2003. The BBFC requested substantial cuts (1m 23s) before granting an '18' certificate, 'to remove instructive detail of illegal drug use'.

Italian movie mogul Carlo Ponti hired Pink Floyd to score *Zabriskie Point* (1970), co-written and directed by Michelangelo Antonioni. This $7 million film was produced by Metro-Goldwyn-Mayer, which hoped to cash in on *Easy Rider* (1969) with its own counter-culture hit. Pink Floyd's songs for *Zabriskie Point* included 'Crumbling Land', which at least captured the theme of a disintegrating society. Antonioni also used tracks by The Rolling Stones, The Grateful Dead, John Fahey, Kaleidoscope and The Youngbloods. Against the director's wishes, MGM boss James Aubrey closed the film with 'So Young', a song by *protege* Mike Curb. Intended as a critique of modern America, *Zabriskie Point* proved a critical and commercial disaster, grossing under $1 million in the United States. Co-star dismissed the film as 'a big lie and totally alien'.

Pink Floyd reunited with Barbet Schroeder for *La Vallee* (1972), aka *The Valley Obscured by Clouds*. This French production involved a multi-national group of hippies searching for a lost valley – and themselves – in Papua, New Guinea. Schroeder intended the film to be dream-like and esoteric. According to actor Jean-Pierre Kalfon, the cast and crew spent three months in the jungles of New Guinea. During filming, Schroeder and his actors met the Mapuga tribe, which had had no contact with white civilisation until the 1950s. Star Bulle Ogier was the first white woman to meet the Mapuga, a moment recorded on film. Some of the actors took part in tribal rituals, stripping naked to be covered with ceremonial body paint.

Schroeder claims to have chosen Pink Floyd for the score because the actors listened to the band's music. Schroeder gave Pink Floyd a few ideas about what he wanted, then left them to get on with it. The tracks for *La Vallee* were recorded at the Chateau d'Herouville, in France, under the supervision of sound engineer Dominique Bleufeutare. According to Bleufeutare, Pink Floyd seemed frustrated by the technical limitations of the time. The songs included 'Obscured By Clouds' and 'Free Four'. Interviewed a decade later, David Gilmour cited *La Vallee* as one of Roger Waters' inspirations for the *Wall* concept. 'Free Fall' reflected on the death of his father, Eric Fletcher Waters, killed in the Second World War. Schroeder also felt the whole film had thematic similarities with *The Wall*, touching on the nature of the self and the longing for death.

La Vallee opened in France on 6 July 1972, to mixed reviews. While Nestor Almendros'

Roger Daltrey as the
pinball wizard in Ken
Russell's *Tommy* (1975)

location photography drew praise, critics dismissed the film as clichéd and superficial. Many Pink Floyd fans felt there wasn't enough of the band's music. Schroeder used only excerpts from songs on the *Valley* album. Jean-Pierre Kalfon, himself a musician, later admitted to disliking the Pink Floyd sound. In 1980, Schroeder caught up with Pink Floyd while the band was performing *The Wall* in Los Angeles. Schroeder described the show as the most moving he'd ever seen.

The year after *La Vallee*, Pink Floyd produced their definitive concert movie, *Pink Floyd Live at Pompeii* (1973). Written, directed and edited by Adrian Maben, the film centered on Pink Floyd performing in the otherwise empty Pompeii amphitheatre. There were also interviews with the group, backstage footage and many shots of the spectacular Pompeii landscape. The Pompeii concert sequences were filmed in October 1971. Additional songs were shot in a Paris film studio, where Maben completed the blue screen work needed for several Pompeii scenes. The final cut featured rhythmic editing, hypnotically slow zooms and the briefly fashionable split-screen technique. Popular with fans, *Live at Pompeii* received lukewarm reviews. *Time Out* critic Scott Meek praised the film's technical accomplishment while questioning its worth: 'The film may be a brilliant visual record of the Floyd playing, but sadly the music works on you more if you just close your eyes.' Apparently, *Live at Pompeii* became a cult hit in France, playing at Paris cinemas well into the 1980s. The band's music was also heard in *Crystal Voyager* (David Elfick, 1972), a surfing epic, and an episode of the television series *Cosmos* (1980).

While Pink Floyd notched up a fair collection of film credits, they had never made a 'pop star movie' as such. The 1970s proved a relatively sparse period for such British films. The glam rock group Slade made a creditable debut in *Flame* (1974), a sour take on the music industry. Scripted by Andrew Birkin, the film underwent heavy cutting to avoid an 'X' rating in the UK. Led Zeppelin contributed *The Song Remains the Same* (1976), a mixture of documentary, concert footage and fantasy sequences. Peter Frampton and The Bee Gees signed on for the American-made *Sgt Pepper's Lonely Hearts Club Band* (1978), a movie based on someone else's concept album. Guest appearances from Alice Cooper, David Bowie, Aerosmith and Earth, Wind and Fire didn't help. The Sex Pistols rounded off the decade with *The Great Rock'n'Roll Swindle* (1979), made after the pioneering punk band disintegrated. Written and directed by Julian Temple, the film was dominated by 'host' Malcolm McLaren, the Pistols' creator-manager.

The most obvious forerunner for *Pink Floyd The Wall* was *Tommy* (1975), based on The Who's 1969 concept album. This mystical rock opera starred Who lead singer Roger Daltrey, with support from Elton John, Eric Clapton and Tina Turner. Directed by Ken Russell, *Tommy* was co-produced by Hemdale and the Robert Stigwood Organisation, with distribution through Columbia. With an eye to the box-office, Russell and Stigwood recruited a number of 'name' actors: Oliver Reed, Ann-Margret, Robert Powell and Jack Nicholson. *Tommy* has been criticised as crass, overblown and simplistic, despite Russell's undeniable visual flair.

Released on 27 March 1975, *Tommy* scored a box-office success and some favourable reviews. Writing in the *Sunday Times*, Dilys Powell seemed bemused: 'You are left with a dream-plot; with music which as I heard it seemed hysterical; and with the purgatorial shapes which Mr Russell has used to interpret an original already half-spectral...it swells from fantasy to nightmare.' Powell praised Roger Daltrey's performance as the title character, 'astonishingly ranging from silent vacancy to bawling confidence'. On balance, Powell felt Russell's self-indulgence could be forgiven: 'I am inclined to think that Mr Russell has used the blinding, deafening music to let himself blindingly and deafeningly go. All the same one can't drag one's eyes away from the screen. Let's face it, nothing he does is without ferocious interest.' Alexander Walker saw *Tommy* as a personal triumph for the director: 'Undoubtedly his best film of the decade...One feels inside a mind which has blown every rational fuse: for once, one feels at home with Ken Russell.' Budgeted at $5.5 million, *Tommy* took $17.7 million at the North American box-office. There were Academy Award nominations for Ann-Margret, cast as Tommy's mother, and the adapted score.

In the autumn of 1980, Roger Waters approached the film division of Pink Floyd's British record company EMI with *The Wall* concept. Already a best-selling album and equally popular stage show, *The Wall* looked like a solid movie property. Waters envisaged the *Wall* film as a mixture of concert footage, animation, dramatised scenes and fantasy sequences. From the start, however, EMI seemed dubious about the project. Despite the success of *Tommy*, filmed rock operas were hardly an established popular genre. Unlike *Tommy*, *The Wall* didn't offer big movie names such as Ann-Margret, Jack Nicholson or even Oliver Reed. In November 1980, EMI turned down *The Wall*, explaining: 'This is something we can't do right now.' Taken aback, Waters realised he needed an influential ally within the film industry. He approached writer-director Alan Parker, one of the few British filmmakers with an international profile.

Born in Islington, London, in 1944, Alan Parker got his first break in advertising. On leaving school, Parker joined an advertising agency as an office boy. Working for several agencies, he was eventually promoted to copywriter. In the mid-sixties, Parker met David Puttnam, an advertising executive and would-be film producer. At the time, both men worked for the Collett, Dickinson and Pearce (CDP) agency. A respected writer, Parker expressed an interest in developing screenplays. While Parker and Puttnam were keen to branch into feature films, their initial plans came to nothing. Unwilling to work on a cigarette advertising campaign, Puttnam left CDP, setting up his own photographic agency. Parker graduated to directing television commercials.

In 1970, Alan Parker established a production company with colleague Alan Marshall. Active in the British film industry for some years, Marshall would become Parker's regular producer. The company proved a major success, turning into one of Britain's leading commercial production houses. Parker made a name for himself directing a series of slick commercials. While the best known features Elgar's New World Symphony and Hovis sliced bread, Parker also promoted Birds Eye products, Supermousse and good old fashioned milk. A big movie fan, Parker liked to include film references in his adverts, paying *homage* to David Lean's *Brief Encounter* (1945) and *Oliver Twist* (1948), among others. Parker would direct over 600 commercials. His regular team included Welsh cameraman Peter Biziou.

In 1968, David Puttnam had founded the film company Goodtimes Enterprises, in partnership with American producer Sanford Lieberson. Parker wrote the screenplay for the Goodtimes production *Melody* (1971), a teenage love triangle romance directed by Waris Hussein. Also known as *S.W.A.L.K.* (Sealed With A Loving Kiss), the film reunited *Oliver!* stars Mark Lester and Jack Wild. Puttnam had commissioned the script from Parker back in 1966, paying his copywriter friend the princely sum of £500. *Melody* was made in association with Seagrams, a US distillation company, and the Hemdale Corporation, a production-distribution outfit founded by actor David Hemmings and his business partner John Daly. Featuring tracks by Crosby, Stills and Nash and The Bee Gees, *Melody* is a sentimental fantasy, despite the 'realistic' backdrop. David Puttnam refers to the film as 'the *Jules et Jim* of the nappy set'. *Melody* made effective use of several South London locations, familiar to both Parker and Puttnam from their childhoods. Lester and Wild contribute solid performances, as does Tracy Hyde, cast as Lester's girlfriend. Budgeted at a modest $600,000, *Melody* did well in the United States and Far East territories.

Alan Parker made his feature directing debut with *Bugsy Malone* (1976), a curious gangster musical which he also scripted. The film was co-produced by David Puttnam. Since *Melody*, Goodtimes had enjoyed further success with *That'll Be the Day* (1973) and *Stardust* (1974), featuring singer David Essex as a John Lennon-style pop star. On the downside, movies such as *The Pied Piper* (1971), starring Donovan, *The Final Programme* (1974) and *Mahler* (1974) barely recovered their costs. Goodtimes crashed and burned with *Lisztomania* (1975), Ken Russell's ill-conceived follow-up to *Tommy*. Puttnam and Russell blame each other for this costly flop, which damaged both their careers. For *Bugsy Malone*, Puttnam and Parker set up Bugsy Malone Productions. Attracting minimal finance from Paramount and Rank, they had to mortgage their homes to meet the budget. Parker's crew included cameraman Peter Biziou. The cast, led by Scott Baio and Jodie Foster, was made up entirely of children. *Bugsy Malone* proved a successful pastiche of 1930s gangster movies, with pedal-operated getaway cars and 'splurge' guns that fire whipped cream. American composer Paul Williams supplied an appealing score, with only occasional lapses into cuteness. It probably helped that the songs were dubbed by adult performers. In Britain, the critical response to *Bugsy Malone* ranged from enthusiasm to puzzlement. The film received mixed reviews in the crucial United States market.

Parker scored his first big international success with *Midnight Express* (1978), where a young American tourist convicted of drug smuggling experiences the hell of a Turkish prison. Based on the true story of Billy Hayes, the film was distributed by Columbia Pictures. While *Midnight Express* can be criticised as manipulative, unsubtle and simplistic, the film has undeniable force. Oliver Stone's script made several departures from Hayes' version of events. Significantly, the film renders Hayes a more sympathetic figure, despite his drug use. David Puttnam, who co-produced the film, felt he'd misjudged audience reaction to several key scenes. Hayes' acts of violence, intended to be shocking, had viewers applauding. Writing in *Time*, Richard Schickel attacked *Midnight Express* as 'One of the ugliest sado-masochistic trips…that our thoroughly nasty movie age has yet produced.' Nevertheless, *Midnight Express* scored a major box-office success. Budgeted at $2.3 million, the film took $35 million in the United States alone. Despite the controversy, *Midnight Express* also received Academy Award nominations for Best Picture, Best Director, Best Adapted Screenplay, Best Supporting Actor (John Hurt) and Best Score. Oliver Stone won an Oscar, as did composer Giorgio Moroder. Parker and Hurt were compensated with British Academy Awards.

Alan Parker made his American debut with *Fame* (1980), a musical based around New York's High School for Performing Arts, in Manhattan. An ethnically diverse group of students attempt to live their dreams, experiencing heartbreak, triumph and dancing in the street. As Parker explained, 'Our film, I hope, will be a microcosm of New York… a dozen races pitching in and having their own crack at the American dream.' Though patchy and episodic, *Fame* benefited from Parker's energetic direction. Composer Michael Gore won Academy Awards for his score and the title song. *Fame* later became a soft-centred television series, featuring original cast members Lee Curreri, Gene Anthony Ray, Debbie Allen and Albert Hague. Parker attempted a more heavyweight drama with *Shoot the Moon* (1981),

Director Alan Parker with Diane Keaton
on the set of *Shoot the Moon* (1982)

a California tale of family break-up and possible reconciliation.

When Roger Waters first contacted Alan Parker, the director was still busy with *Shoot the Moon*. Initially, Waters simply asked Parker to help find another backer for *The Wall*. Waters didn't intend Parker to be directly involved with the movie, as Parker explains: 'I was really there to encourage him [Waters] to make it as a film, not for me to make it as a film. And to advise Roger in not getting involved with the wrong people in film, a world that he didn't know.' Parker then discussed the *Wall* project with various film executives, only to face the same rejection as Waters.

Waters intended to make *The Wall* in association with Gerald Scarfe, who had co-designed both the album and the stage show. Scarfe's ultimate role on the film would be as designer and supervising director of the animated scenes. Crediting Scarfe with 'a wonderfully strange brain', Parker felt the cartoonist's work had 'a weird psychopathic quality', well suited to the film.

In the meantime, Waters developed the album's ideas and images into a screenplay

Waters had assumed that his script would be revised by a professional screenwriter, but Parker assured him this wasn't necessary. According to Alan Marshall, Parker worked on the script himself, especially the imagery. The end result ran to only 35-39 pages.

In February 1981, Waters, Scarfe and Parker put together a 70 page book, outlining the movie, to show potential backers. Meeting at Scarfe's home in Cheyne Walk, Chelsea, London, the three men spent weeks discussing the material and layouts. Printed in large A3 format, the lavish, full-colour guide featured complete song lyrics, 50 Gerald Scarfe illustrations, 17 photographs of Pink Floyd in concert and 29 excerpts from the screenplay. As the introduction explained, 'The presentation is a visual aid to understanding both how

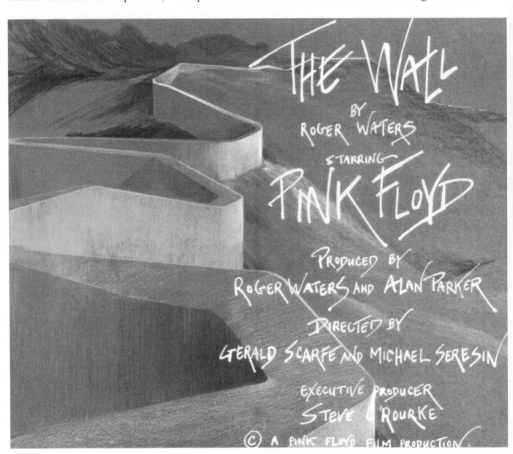

the film will be made, and how it will look when finished.'

The credits listed Pink Floyd as the stars, with Waters and Parker co-producing. At this stage, directorial responsibilities were still to be split between Gerald Scarfe and Michael Seresin, Parker's regular director of photography. The New Zealand-born Seresin had been active in British films since the late 1960s, working on *If...* (1968) as an assistant cameraman. Like Parker, Seresin found his big break in television commercials, both as cameraman and director. Seresin quickly became a major figure in the field, wining over 40 industry awards. Having co-photographed *Bugsy Malone* with Peter Biziou, Seresin remained with Parker for *Midnight Express*, *Fame* and *Shoot the Moon*.

The outline for *Pink Floyd The Wall* is more coherent than the film eventually made, the ideas behind the concept clearly explained. As the foreword puts it, '*The Wall* is a musical biography of a character called Pink. Pink is a fictional character created to represent a rock group like Pink Floyd... using a combination of narrative, live action and animation we are able to tell Pink's story to even greater effect than was possible in concert'. The recurring imagery includes 'swirling mists, twisted metal and barbed wire'. Despite the introduction of Pink, much of the film centred on Pink Floyd. The 'Happiest Days Of Our Lives' sequence would begin with Roger Waters singing, before turning into an animated sequence. 'Mother' was planned as a concert performance, using the inflatable puppet from the stage show, with new giant arms. The more cinematic elements reflected Waters' inexperience with the medium. 'Comfortably Numb' featured Pink 'kneed in the balls by anonymous people on tube trains'. Sadly, this image didn't make it into the film.

Sequences reworked in the final movie included a banquet, where the Pink Floyd crew enjoy caviar and champagne. Waters and the other band members would appear, as a prelude to 'Hey You'. It's notable that Waters remained the central figure throughout the outline. Gerald Scarfe's rendering of Pink the fascist dictator was clearly based on Waters' features. The film would climax with parallel scenes of symbolic destruction: 'The wall of cardboard bricks in the real gig falls, the stadium in the animation falls, the masks of the followers crack and crumble. The stage in the rally cracks and breaks up. There is a lot of dust and smoke.'

Copies of the outline were distributed to Gilmour and Mason, Steve O'Rourke and concert promoter Harvey Goldsmith. At this point, the plan was to fine-tune the book, presenting the finished version at a meeting for potential investors. Scarfe's illustrations included drawings of O'Rourke and Goldsmith. According to rumour, Goldsmith disliked his caricatured image and asked for it to be removed. Around 100 copies of the finished book were printed.

Roger Waters subsequently produced a new draft of the screenplay, dated 8 May 1981.

Alan Parker with Bob Geldof,
the star of *Pink Floyd The Wall*

Running just under 40 pages, this revised version is much closer to the final movie, with far fewer concert-based sequences. Whatever Parker's involvement with the script, Waters retained sole writing credit. The slender screenplay was accompanied by complete song lyrics and nearly 90 drawings.

Waters intended to include five songs from Pink Floyd's forthcoming Earl's Court performances. As Parker explained, 'The concert was still the most powerful thing that we all had in our mind from a visual point of view.' For example, 'The Thin Ice' would begin with darkness, slowly revealing the beginnings of the wall. David Gilmour had his doubts, feeling the Earls Court venue was unsatisfactory from an acoustic point of view.

Technical problems meant that the footage shot by Scarfe and Seresin had to be adandoned. In any case, Parker had no interest in making a concert movie, as he explained during shooting:

'we wanted it to be totally cinematic, a film in its own right'. After reviewing the footage, Waters agreed that none of it would fit the movie. Quality aside, he accepted that the concert footage would jar with the animation and staged live action. Waters and Gerald Scarfe still wanted to use a number of elements from the *Wall* stage show. Parker persuaded them that this approach would be too theatrical. As a music fan, Parker conceded that the actual show had considerable merit: 'in theatrical terms and audience terms, it was a complete success'. Having struck out with the concert footage, Michael Seresin left the project. From this point on, the only director connected to *The Wall* was Alan Parker himself.

As the guiding force behind *The Wall*, Roger Waters intended to play the role of Pink himself. Following a screen test, Parker is rumoured to have told Waters to his face that he couldn't act. Parker also suggested that Waters was too close to the material to be comfortable playing Pink. It soon became clear that *The Wall* would be a rock movie without the actual rock stars in it.

Parker had realised early on that *The Wall* wouldn't get made with Roger Waters in the lead. Alan Marshall felt the role of Pink was hard to cast, with few obvious choices. In Marshall's view, Pink had to be played by someone with 'a decent rock and roll voice'. Ironically, Waters was replaced by another pop star with no previous film experience. With an eye to the youth market, the producers cast Bob Geldof, lead singer of The Boomtown Rats, a successful Irish New Wave-Punk act. While The Boomtown Rats were never serious rivals to The Sex Pistols, The Clash or The Buzzcocks, they enjoyed number one hits with 'Rat Trap' and 'I Don't Like Mondays'. Geldof had strong features, undeniable presence and an aggressive attitude.

When the producers contacted Bob Geldof's agent, the singer initially seemed uninterested. Aside from his lack of acting experience, he didn't like Pink Floyd's music. Roger Waters recalled Geldof's exact words as 'Pink Floyd, load of crap!' Geldof wasn't the only punk generation star to hold psychedelic progressive rock in contempt. John Lydon, aka Johnny Rotten, claims he was recruited for The Sex Pistols on the strength of his t-shirt, which bore the legend 'I hate Pink Floyd'. According to Geldof, he first heard about the film while riding in a taxi with his agent. By an incredible coincidence, the driver happened to be Roger Waters' brother, who informed his sibling of Geldof's negative response. Geldof's manager persuaded him to look at the script, arguing that *The Wall* would be good for his career. Finally, Geldof agreed to make a screen test. Alan Parker asked him to act out an emotional courtroom scene from *Midnight Express*. Parker was impressed with Geldof's performance, rating the test a big success. Parker showed the scene to the members of Pink Floyd. David Gilmour felt Geldof 'was a good choice' for Pink, describing the test as 'brilliant'. According to Alan Marshall,

Waters remained doubtful. Parker had to convince Waters that Geldof was the best choice. Eventually, Geldof agreed to play the role. Whatever his feelings about the *Wall* project, Geldof had been considering a movie career for some time. As he explained: 'I wanted to make a film. I'd the time and I thought it was too good an opportunity to miss, working with Alan Parker, Gerald Scarfe and Roger Waters.' In Parker's view, casting Geldof brought 'a freshness and a new life' to the character of Pink. Geldof received a special 'introducing' credit on the movie, often the kiss of death for an aspiring star. By way of compensation, Waters took additional producer credits on the music and animation sequences. He also made a cameo appearance, uncredited, as a witness at Pink's registry office wedding.

With Bob Geldof cast as Pink, Alan Parker finally secured a deal with American major Metro-Goldwyn-Mayer, which backed *Fame* and *Shoot the Moon*. Apparently, MGM agreed to make the film without ever seeing the painstakingly prepared outline. While MGM agreed to finance *The Wall*, the studio struck a hard bargain, Pink Floyd underwriting the final cost. Parker assembled a high calibre team for the film, including producer Alan Marshall, who worked on *Bugsy Malone*, *Midnight Express*, *Fame* and *Shoot the Moon*. For *The Wall*, Parker and Marshall worked through the Goldcrest company. At the time, Goldcrest was riding high on the success of *Chariots of Fire* (1981), a personal triumph for producer David Puttnam.

Steve O'Rourke served as an executive producer on *The Wall*. O'Rourke had already taken this role on *The Odd Job* (1978), a vehicle for *Monty Python* star Graham Chapman, who also served as co-producer and co-writer. After a troubled preproduction, the film emerged as a misfiring black comedy, poorly reviewed and barely released. The associate producer on *The Wall* was Garth Thomas, a long-time Alan Parker associate. Thomas had served as a production manager on *Our Cissy*, *Footsteps*, *Bugsy Malone* and *Midnight Express*. His other credits included *The Pied Piper*, *That'll Be the Day*, *Stardust*, *Flame*, *The Last Remake of Beau Geste* (1977) and *Alien* (1979).

Parker also recruited cameraman Peter Biziou, production designer Brian Morris and editor Gerry Hambling. For *The Wall*, Morris shared responsibilities with Gerald Scarfe, who took credit as the overall designer. Active in films since the 1950s, Gerry Hambling edited *Bugsy Malone*, *Midnight Express*, *Fame* and *Shoot the Moon*. The choreography was entrusted to Gillian Gregory, whose extensive film credits included *Tommy* and *Quadrophenia* (1979), The Who's second attempt at a rock'n'roll movie. Gregory had also worked on *Mahler*, *Valentino* (1977), *Shock Treatment* (1981) and *Reds* (1981). Conceived as a big movie, *The Wall* would be shot in 35mm Panavision – offering an ultra-wide image – with a Dolby soundtrack. For showcase venues, the producers decided to use 70mm prints with six-track sound.

Unlike *Tommy*, *The Wall* had little in the way of star cameos. The biggest name in the film was Bob Hoskins, cast as Pink's manager. Hoskins had achieved television stardom in Dennis Potter's *Pennies from Heaven* (1978), an equally downbeat musical drama. Hoskins had given a star-calibre performance in *The Long Good Friday* (1980), playing a doomed East End gangster. The only other well known face was James Hazeldine, who made his film debut in the downbeat epic *Nicholas and Alexandra* (1971), cast as the young Stalin. A stage actor by inclination, Hazeldine also appeared in *The Ruling Class* (1972), *The National Health*, opposite Bob Hoskins, *Stardust* and *The Medusa Touch* (1978). Pink's Mother was played by Christine Hargreaves, seen in *The Reckoning* (1969), *The Hireling* (1973), *It Shouldn't Happen to a Vet* (1975) and *An American Werewolf in London* (1981). The role of Pink's Father went to James Laurenson, whose film work included *Women in Love* (1969), *Assault* (1971) and *The Monster Club* (1980). Pink's Wife was played by newcomer Eleanor David, who had to strip off for the role, joining James Hazeldine for some artfully shot humping.

Alan Parker needed a child actor to play the young Pink. Rather than search the various stage schools, he decided to use a non-professional, as the role required little 'acting' as such. Parker held open casting calls in London, Leeds, Manchester and Glasgow, seeing thousands of candidates. He eventually settled on Kevin McKeon, who had a natural, unselfconscious screen presence. Ironically, McKeon had accompanied a friend to the audition, only trying for the part himself at the last minute.

The Wall featured several high class actors in non-speaking bit parts. Pink's roadies included Phil Davis and Gary Olsen. Davis had appeared in the BBC play *Grown-Ups* (1980), one of several collaborations with writer-director Mike Leigh. Olsen could be seen in *Birth of the Beatles* (1979), *Bloody Kids* (1979), *Breaking Glass* (1980), a vehicle for singer Hazel O'Connor, and *Outland* (1981). A quartet of groupies included cult figure Nell Campbell, also billed as 'Little Nell'. The Australian-born Campbell was best known for playing another groupie – Columbia – in *The Rocky Horror Picture Show* (1975). One of Campbell's fellow groupies was Joanne Whalley, then relatively unknown.

As with *Tommy*, *The Wall* made radical departures from the original album. 'The Thin Ice', 'The Happiest Days of Our Lives', 'Another Brick in the Wall part 2', 'Goodbye Blue Sky' and 'Bring the Boys Back Home' were remixed, some of them in extended versions. 'In the Flesh?', 'Another Brick in the Wall part 3', 'In the Flesh', 'Stop' and 'Outside the Wall' were re-recorded. Bob Geldof sang both 'In the Flesh?' and 'In the Flesh' himself, the former in an extended version. Roger Waters resisted this decision, arguing that Geldof's voice sounded too Irish. As Water's *alter ego*, Pink was supposed to be English, a child of the Second World

War. To preserve this characterisation, Geldof should mime to Waters' vocals. Alan Parker disagreed, winning the argument. Artistic differences aside, it seemed pointless casting a *bona fide* rock star and not using his voice.

'Mother' and 'Empty Spaces' were re-recorded with changed lyrics. Roger Waters felt 'Mother' needed a more narrative-oriented style to work as film music. The lyric 'Is it just a waste of time?' became 'Am I really dying?' Notable, the film offered a chance for Waters to restore 'When The Tigers Broke Free', the 'tigers' of the title given form on screen as German panzers.

The score was orchestrated and conducted by Michael Kamen, who worked on the original album. Trained at New York's Juilliard School, Kamen had been employed in the film business since the early 1970s. His eclectic credits included *Zachariah* (1971), 'the first electric western', *Godspell* (1973), *The Next Man* (1976), *Between the Lines* (1977) and *Polyester* (1981). With an orchestra at his disposal, Kamen could devise fuller, more elaborate arrangements. Kamen and Waters also made use of the Islington Green School Choir and the Pontardulais Male Voice Choir. Michael Kamen went on to become one of Hollywood's most respected composers, scoring *The Dead Zone* (1983), *Brazil* (1985), *Mona Lisa* (1985), *Lethal Weapon* (1987) and *Die Hard* (1988), among others. Kamen died in November 2003, aged 55.

Pink Floyd The Wall began filming on 7 September 1981. Much of *The Wall* was shot at Pinewood Studios and on locations in and around London, including Dulwich College. Roger Waters claimed that Alan Parker always favoured South London locations, as he knew them well from his childhood. The back of Wembley Stadium doubled for an American concert venue. The Anzio war scenes were shot on sand dunes in Barnstable. The classroom sequences were filmed at The Royal Masonic School, in Bushey, Hertfordshire. One location, the Beckton gasworks in East London, later doubled for Vietnam in Stanley Kubrick's *Full Metal Jacket* (1987). For the climactic rally sequence, the production relocated to the Royal Horticultural Hall in Victoria, London. While this wasn't the easiest location, lacking any filming facilities, its Albert Speer-style architecture was perfect for the scene. Rather than hire extras, the producers put out adverts inviting Pink Floyd fans to take part in the crowd scenes.

For Alan Parker, *The Wall* offered a rare opportunity to experiment with a wide variety of visual styles. The Anzio sequences were based on the work of Robert Cappa, a celebrated World War II photographer. The Messerschmidt fighter planes used in these scenes were models, with seven feet wingspans. Though much cheaper than full scale replicas, the planes tended to go out of control, flying off into the distance. For one scene, Parker wanted the camera to track across Pink's wristwatch, hand and cigarette in extreme close-up. Unable to

Parker takes his cameras on to the streets of London to shoot the scenes of skinhead violence

accomplish this with conventional filming techniques, Parker hired Oxford Scientific Films, who shot the footage with special lenses. Normally involved with educational films and documentaries, Oxford Scientific had previously worked with director John Boorman on *Zardoz* (1974), *Exorcist II: The Heretic* (1977) and *Excalibur* (1981).

Bob Geldof approached his first acting role with some trepidation. Alan Parker had confidence in his novice star and Geldof soon got into the film-making process: 'At first I was just embarrassed... but there's a sense of enjoyment overcoming that embarrassment.' Co-star Bob Hoskins kept the working atmosphere light-hearted, making jokes about Cliff Richard. The 'Thin Ice' sequence featured Pink floating in a Los Angeles hotel swimming pool. A non-swimmer, Geldof was kept afloat by a plastic body mould. While the scene was shot indoors,

Camera operator John Stanier, Gerald Scarfe and
Alan Parker on location for *Pink Floyd The Wall*

at Pinewood Studios, the water soon chilled Geldof. Parker encouraged him to be stoical,
'Think how cold Esther Williams must have been', a reference to MGM's swimming star of
the 1940s. There were also problems with the scene where Pink shaves his chest and
eyebrows, blood dripping into the sink. According to Roger Waters, this was something Syd
Barrett had done. Parker didn't realize that Geldof hated the sight of blood, even the fake
variety. While Geldof got through the scene, he found the filming traumatic. Geldof drew the
line at shaving his head, which Waters and Parker felt would add to the effect. Waters' script
had Pink cutting his hair with scissors, then shaving his scalp with a razor, 'clumsily nicking
the flesh'. Geldof only lost his cool once, while filming Pink's 'blob' transformation scene,
where the rock star turns into walking luncheon meat. The sequence was shot at a biscuit
factory in Hammersmith, which lacked any form of heating. Covered in heavy make-up, and

little else, Geldof got extremely cold, blaming Parker for his uncomfortable predicament.

By the end of shooting, Alan Parker had nothing but praise for Geldof, 'I think he's done remarkably well.' Roger Waters conceded that Geldof had been the right choice for Pink, 'He's doing it a hell of a lot better than I ever could have done.' Interviewed before the movie wrapped, Geldof was withholding his verdict: 'As to whether you're any good or not, that's something you have to find out.'

One scene had Pink trashing his hotel room in front of a terrified groupie, played by American actress Jenny Wright. Alan Parker didn't tell Wright that Geldof would throw a wine bottle in her direction. Needless to say, Wright looks genuinely scared in the finished sequence. Pink's orgy of destruction spared the room's lamps, as Gerald Scarfe wanted them for his house. Similarly, the children employed as extras for the school scenes enjoyed trashing and burning their classroom.

The fascist rally and rampage sequences featured real skinheads, who clearly relished their roles. Presumably, the producers had dismissed the options of handing out hundreds of bald head wigs or finding extras willing to shave their heads. In the event, the 380 skinheads employed on *The Wall* proved hard to control. During filming at the Royal Horticultural Hall, cameraman Peter Biziou was up on a balcony, taking light readings. A group of nearby skinheads joked about throwing him off the balcony. While Biziou tried not to take this threat seriously, he found the aggression unsettling. Biziou later remarked that the skinheads were too into their parts. The skinheads also picked on the Pink Floyd fans recruited for the rally scene. In the event, there were only minor skirmishes during the shoot.

The animation sequences for *The Wall* were among the most ambitious ever seen in a British feature film. Gerald Scarfe's key animator was Mike Stuart, who got an early break on *The Beatles* (1965), an animated television series. *The Wall* featured fifteen minutes of animation footage, requiring 10,000 individual drawings. Scarfe and Roger Waters lifted some of the animation from the *Wish You Were Here* and *The Wall* stage shows. The animation artwork had to be adapted from the Academy ratio (1.37:1) to the Panavision format (2.35:1), which presented difficulties. The animated scenes outlined in the concept book included a railway station sequence, where Young Pink looks in vain for his dead father. Parker decided to shoot the scene as live action. Despite his busy schedule, Gerald Scarfe had time to join Parker and Waters for much of the live action filming.

The *Wall* producers commissioned director Barry Chattington to shoot a 'making of...' documentary, *The Other Side of the Wall* (1982). This 25 minute film was narrated by American actor David Healey, presumably a concession to US audiences. According to the portentous voiceover, written by Tim Shackleton, 'What makes *Pink Floyd The Wall* so unusual' was that 'the people right at the creative heart together have brought a new, exciting and uniquely energetic approach to the business of making movies'. The narration also made such bold pronouncements as '*The Wall* is a study of the alienation process' and 'The parallels between today's rock star and much of our recent history are potent and disturbing'.

Pink Floyd The Wall was sold as 'An Alan Parker Film…By Roger Waters'. This contradictory credit gives some indication of the power struggles behind the movie. Parker clashed with Roger Waters and, to a lesser extent, Gerald Scarfe. Waters and Scarfe felt they had a clear concept of the film before Parker came on board. By and large, Waters and Scarfe had worked as kindred spirits on the various incarnations of *The Wall*. Several years older than Waters, Scarfe had vivid childhood memories of the Second World War. He also shared Waters' loathing for the post-war education system. The film's images of schoolchildren on a conveyor belt were based on drawings Scarfe had done for *Punch* magazine, years earlier.

Roger Waters regarded himself as *The Wall*'s true creator, with some justification. Alan Parker, of course, had his own ideas for the film version, which he pushed with enthusiasm. While Parker dismissed the *auteur* theory as a piece of critics' nonsense, he wasn't going to cede his authority as the film's director. If Gerald Scarfe felt sidelined by Parker, Waters saw him as a bitter rival, jostling for position at the helm. Waters always intended *The Wall* as a cult movie, aimed specifically at Pink Floyd's fanbase. In Waters' view, Parker wanted to turn *The Wall* into a mainstream film, losing much of its edge. With two Hollywood movies behind him, Parker was afraid of taking risks. That said, some of Waters' ideas for *The Wall* proved unworkable. For the rally sequence, Waters wanted the crowds' heads to explode under aerial bombardment as they worship Pink. While David Cronenberg had blown up a head to good effect in *Scanners* (1980), it was a hard trick to pull off. Waters eventually accepted that a mass cranial detonation would be unintentionally funny.

Waters spent a lot of time on the *Wall* set, discussing scenes with cast members such as Christine Hargreaves and Kevin McKeon. For Parker, returning to England to make *The Wall* was a risk. If this unconventional project failed, his reputation and career would suffer. With this in mind, Parker had no time for Waters' interference. At one point, Parker demanded that Waters be barred from the set. According to rumour, the director walked off the film on several occasions. David Gilmour acted as a peacemaker, persuading Parker to stay. For all Waters' dallies with the cinema, he couldn't replace Parker, who had five feature films to his name, four as a director. Parker also had a legally binding contract. Interviewed by Robin Denselow in 1988, Gilmour explained that his intervention came at a price. When

Waters proved unwilling to back down, Gilmour sided with Parker: 'I had to go to Roger and say to him 'Give him [Parker] what it says in his contract… otherwise we'll have to have a meeting of the shareholders and directors… and we'll out-vote you.'

The release version of *Pink Floyd The Wall* was assembled from 60 hours of filming. Roger Waters exerted his authority during post-production at Pinewood Studios, still clashing with Alan Parker. 'It was a nightmare,' said Waters in 1990. 'We just screamed and screamed at each other, particularly through the editing of the thing.' Waters worked with James Guthrie on the sound mix for *The Wall*. Taken a reel at a time, the film played well enough, despite being 'a little bit busy'. The full length rough cut was another matter. As Waters explained in 1990: '…when we put all 13 reels together and sat and watched it,

I felt my heart going lower and lower and lower and sank into my boots. I found it almost unwatchable.' He later remarked: 'it was all looking a bit dodgy'. Waters suggested cutting Reel 7, the entire 'Hey You' sequence, which featured riot police battling a rampaging mob, 'The thing was just too long…on it's own it's great.'

According to Waters, Parker didn't protest this decision, feeling the footage was too repetitive. Ironically, stills from the deleted sequence appeared in the obligatory 'book of the film', along with the lyrics. That said, editor Gerry Hambling used around 80 per cent of the 'Hey You' footage for montage sequences elsewhere in the film. According to Parker, the final cut contained around 6000 individual shots.

Alan Parker admitted to being 'drained' by *The Wall*. In *The Other Side of the Wall*, which gives little hint of the production strife, Parker compares the experience to 'going over Victoria Falls in a barrel'. Later on, he put it more bluntly: 'One of the most miserable experiences of my creative life.' Roger Waters described the filming as 'a very unnerving and unpleasant experience…we all fell out in a big way.'

For all the arguments and ego clashes, *Pink Floyd The Wall* is a technically accomplished, visually striking piece of work. At the time, Alan Parker remarked: 'Hopefully, we might have made something that's nobody's ever done before.' In many respects, Parker achieved his goal. As an exorcism of Roger Waters' personal demons, *The Wall* has some resonance. As a study of mental breakdown, the film is sometimes simplistic and glib. Rendering Waters' ideas and lyrics into literal images produced mixed results. As Waters pointed out, the relentless barrage of sound and image is both exhausting and alienating: 'I found it was so unremitting in its onslaught upon the senses, that it didn't actually give me, anyway, as an audience, a chance to get involved with it.' Waters also feels that *The Wall* is 'deeply flawed' by a lack of humour. Alan Parker later described *The Wall* as 'the most expensive student film ever made'.

Alan Parker intended *The Wall* to be 'very unconventional, very revolutionary'. Parker employs his usual slick style, making good use of Steadicam shots. The film opens with the camera gliding down an empty hotel corridor, an obvious nod to *The Shining* (1980), another study of violent mental breakdown. Parker also favours extreme close-ups, the minutiae of Pink's hotel room taking on immense significance. Like most of Parker's work, *The Wall* is hardly subtle, inter-cutting rampaging fans with charging soldiers. The soundtrack features backwards messages which, when reversed, mention Old Pink, from the Funny Farm, Chalfont. On the downside, there is too much repetition of footage, presumably for budgetary reasons.

From the start, *The Wall* is clearly a film with Something to Say, even if the message isn't

immediately obvious. As *The Other Side of the Wall* put it, 'the themes and symbols employed in *Pink Floyd The Wall* are rich and complex'. Parker fills the screen with chains, locks, pools of blood, clutching hands, blank faces, writhing maggots and the wall itself. Aside from Pink's mental wall, Roger Waters' script also referred to 'The wall of post war reindustrialisation.' In Waters' view, humanity had been crushed by the endless cycle of production and consumption. The anti-authority slant is straightforward, pitting Pink and his fans against vindictive teachers and police brutality. American cops harass fans arriving at a concert, making random arrests and beating up anyone who resists.

Hiding out in his hotel room, Pink slumps in front of the television, watching *The Dam Busters* (1954), a romanticised take on World War II. This footage was not meant to be ironic, Roger Waters praising the film as 'a wonderful heroic story'. While Waters admitted to having

119

an obsession with the film, he conceded that it meant little to non-British audiences. The 8 May 1981 script draft features one scene from *The Dam Busters*, where mission leader Guy Gibson (Richard Todd) learns that his beloved black Labrador has been run over and killed. Unfortunately, the dog is called 'Nigger', prompting some awkward redubbing – to 'Digger' – in recent television versions of the film. According to Waters, the US version of *The Dam Busters* rechristened the dog as 'Trigger'.

The *Wall* outline had Pink watching *Battle of Britain* (1969), extracts from which had featured on the album. Originally, the war movie footage heralded a musical sequence: '…in his deranged state, Pink conjures up a chorus of service men and women with whom he sings to purge himself of his guilty feelings'. Pink also sits through a *Tom and Jerry* cartoon, *The Postman Always Rings Twice* (1946) and *King Solomon's Mines* (1950), presumably because distributor MGM owned the rights.

The *Wall*'s autobiographical elements, such as the father killed in World War II, are sometimes touching. Suffocated by his clinging, overprotective mother, Young Pink retreats into a fantasy world. A lonely child, Pink plays with his father's army uniform and equipment, as Roger Waters did. Pink finds a box of bullets, placing them on a railway track to be detonated by a passing train. In the outline, Pink simply places a one pence piece on the track, to be squashed by the train wheels. Waters admits to having done this himself. The 'Happiest Days Of Our Lives' sequence sees Pink oppressed by the education system. The outline describes Pink's face transforming into 'a round pink mask, his fear expressed by amorphous black shapes representing the wide eye and slack jaw of terror'. Pink's poem, mocked by his sadistic teacher (Alex McAvoy), is actually the second verse of 'Money', from *Dark Side of the Moon*. When the teacher dismisses the lyrics as 'absolute rubbish', fans can sneer at his blinkered ignorance. The supporting characters tend towards stereotypes. In the original outline, Pink's Wife is described as 'a childhood sweetheart', chosen by Pink because 'she is conveniently available'. In the movie, she lacks even this sketchy background.

The Wall has been accused of self-indulgence, Roger Waters and Alan Parker taking equal shares of the blame. Some of the visuals are reminiscent of *Tommy*, another film screaming for attention. Both movies feature wartime sequences and a smattering of Christ allegory. For the record, Bob Geldof is a more convincing martyr figure than Roger Daltrey. Parker also employs some David Cronenberg-style body horror and hallucinogenic visuals out of *Altered States* (1980), one of Ken Russell's better post-*Tommy* films. *The Wall*'s best known images include children fed into the mincing machine of the school system, which crushes any sense of individuality. Waters intended this sequence as part-*homage* to Fritz Lang's *Metropolis*

(1926), where workers in a futuristic city are both dwarfed and dehumanised by their mechanised environment.

Interviewed years later, Roger Waters dismissed *The Wall* as a failure: 'I was a bit disappointed with it in the end, because at the end of the day I felt no sympathy at all with the lead character.' As Pink, Bob Geldof is more a presence than an actor, first identified by his Mickey Mouse wristwatch and heavy stubble. Geldof's dialogue amounts to little more than 'Take that, fuckers!', screamed by Pink as the hotel room is wasted. Geldof does the trashing with conviction. For some viewers, Pink's excruciating shaving scene is the most memorable. As a character, Pink comes across as selfish, self-absorbed and infantile. It comes as no surprise when Pink's estranged wife begins an affair, with a CND campaigner (James

Young Pink (Kevin McKeon) waits for a father who will never return as the crowd sing 'Bring The Boys Back Home'

Hazeldine). Pink's wife later turns into a monstrous insectivore *vagina dentate*, designed by Gerald Scarfe. Forced to share Pink's skewed view of the world, viewers are denied the chance to question his perspective on events. While the other characters speak, we only hear snippets of conversation. Even Bob Hoskins, the biggest name in the film, has to make do with 'Fuck me!'

The animated scenes in *The Wall* received more praise than the live action. The images devised by Scarfe include Pink's screaming face, an obvious *homage* to Edvard Munch's 'The Scream'. The marching hammers, monster teacher and bum-faced judge all featured on the album's sleeve art, reappearing in the stage show. Like Alan Parker, Scarfe has little time for subtlety. Early on in the film, the dove of peace is ripped apart by the German eagle of war. The blatant sexual symbolism is typified by the copulating flowers. Elsewhere, blood runs into a drain as British soldiers are cut down by German machine guns.

The live action scenes of *The Wall* culminate with the fascist rally sequence, complete with shaved heads, black shirts and crossed hammer motif. Fascist Pink is an embodiment of Roger Waters' sense of alienation during the 'In The Flesh' tour. According to the script, 'The set should look like an unholy marriage between Nuremberg in 1936, Red Square on May Day, and a Ku Klux Klan meeting.' Alan Parker described the sequence as 'rock and roll Nuremberg'. There are also some Wagneresque touches, plus a hint of *Triumph of the Will*. Bob Geldof's rendition of the song compares favourably with the Waters original. Fascist Pink attacks gays, Jews, blacks, dopeheads and anyone with spots, screaming for them to go 'up against the wall'. According to Waters' original outline: 'As the rally reaches its climax, Pink suddenly realises he has become an ally to the very forces of tyranny which killed his own father. This proves too much for the core of human feeling within him and he rebels.' As staged by Parker, the sequence loses this point completely.

Pink's self-loathing leads to his animated 'trial', presided over by the bloated judge. This grotesque figure is, as the script says, 'a huge asshole on legs wearing a judge's wig'. Roger Waters intended this climactic animation set-piece as the most extreme in *The Wall*: 'The judge squats on the cylinder and shits images of his [Pink's] past life on him, whilst screaming at him to tear down the wall.' The film tones down the scatology, presumably to avoid offending both the distributor and the censor. The live action coda – not in Waters' script – has no obvious connection to Pink's trial. *The Wall* ends on a freeze-frame, as a small boy pours away the petrol from an unused Molotov cocktail. This is clearly an expression of hope for a more peaceful future.

Pink Floyd The Wall received its world premiere at the 1982 Cannes Film Festival, shown out of competition. On 1 May 1982, David Gilmour and Nick Mason were interviewed for Radio Free Europe, based in France. Gilmour, who spoke fluent French, did most of the talking. They were joined by Barbet Schroeder, the director of *More* and *La Vallee*, and actor-musician Jean-Pierre Kalfon, who appeared in the latter. One DJ suggested that *The Wall* was about claustrophobia, isolation and introspection. Gilmour agreed, mentioning Roger Waters' semi-autobiographical approach. Gilmour also explained that the film told the same story as the album and show, in a very different way. The presenters held a series of competitions, offering as prizes four free passes – eight tickets – to the Cannes screening of *The Wall*. Gilmour mentioned that he hoped to attend the premiere, if he could also get in free. Under the circumstances, he may not have been joking. The first competition involved naming as many Pink Floyd soundtracks as possible. The winner, Christophe Legan from Gennevillers, came up with six. Later questions were markedly easier, such as naming two earlier Alan Parker films.

The producers arranged a midnight screening of *The Wall* at Cannes, heightening the sense of an 'event' movie. Unimpressed with the standard cinema speakers, the technicians played the sound through a concert PA system, bringing the volume up to gig level. When the movie went on general release in London and Los Angeles, James Guthrie added sub-woofers to the sound systems of first run theatres. The British Board of Film Censors passed the film uncut with an 'AA' rating – over fourteens only – on 23 June 1982.

Sold with the tagline 'The Memories The Madness The Music…The Movie', *Pink Floyd The Wall* opened in the United Kingdom on 14 July 1982. Whatever Waters and Parker's hopes, the reviews were largely negative. Writing in the *Monthly Film Bulletin*, Steve Jenkins was scathing: 'A vacuous, bombastic and humourless piece of self-indulgence.' According to *Sight and Sound*: 'Roger Waters flounders in woman-hating self-pity; Gerard Scarfe turns up particularly weedy examples of his animated savagery; and Alan Parker revels in the chance to make a feature–length TV commercial.' *Time Out* critic Paul Taylor expressed surprise that Waters and Parker had experienced creative differences. In his view, the film was a triumph of 'stunning literalism…little more than kinetic sleeve art keyed slavishly to a slim concept-album narrative…pictorial italicizing of Waters' lyrics'. Describing Waters as a 'Floydian self-analyst', Taylor felt the film suffered from a 'misogynist petulance'. Summing up, Taylor dismissed *The Wall* as a risible failure: 'Crossing *Privilege* with *Tommy* couldn't result in anything shallower. All in all, it's just another flick to appal.'

In the United States, *The Wall* was released on 6 August 1982. The Motion Picture Association of America gave the film an 'R' (Restricted) rating, limiting its box-office potential. Few teenage fans would want to see *The Wall* accompanied by the obligatory parent or guardian. Nevertheless, the film grossed a respectable $22.24 million at the US box-office. Critic Leonard Maltin, well known for his long-running movie guide, had problems with *The Wall*: '…perhaps the longest rock video to date, and certainly the most depressing'. In South Korea, *The Wall* was initially banned by the censor, emerging nine years later as a cut '18' video release. Fans didn't see the complete version – legally – until 1999. *The Wall* received some industry recognition at the 1983 British Academy of Film and Television Awards (BAFTA), winning trophies for Best Original Song (Roger Waters/'Another Brick in the Wall') and Best Sound (James Guthrie, Eddy Joseph, Clive Winter, Graham V Hartstone, Nicolas Le Messurier).

A solid commercial success, *Pink Floyd The Wall* made little difference to the careers of those involved. Production company Goldcrest later collapsed after the triple failures of *Revolution* (1985), *Absolute Beginners* (1986) and *The Mission* (1986). Alan Parker returned to the United States, enjoying success – and controversy – with *Birdy* (1984), *Angel Heart* (1987) and *Mississippi Burning* (1988). Parker also drew praise for the Irish-themed films *The Commitments* (1991) and *Angela's Ashes* (1999). Parker's only subsequent musical was *Evita* (1996), starring Madonna as Eva Peron. Though smoothly assembled, this long-gestating film project magnified the flaws of the Andrew Lloyd Webber-Tim Rice stage show.

While Parker and producer Alan Marshall parted company after *Angel Heart*, the director reunited with cameraman Peter Biziou for *Mississippi Burning*. Bizou received an Academy Award for his work on this Deep South drama of racial hatred, based on a 1964 murder case. Production designer Brian Morris worked with Parker on *Angel Heart*, *The Commitments*, *The Road to Wellville* (1994) and *Evita*. Editor Gerry Hambling is still a regular Parker collaborator, most recently on *The Life of David Gale* (2003).

Of the *Wall* cast, Bob Hoskins drew Hollywood interest, receiving an Academy Award nomination for his performance in *Mona Lisa* (1985). Hoskins later co-starred in the American-made *Who Framed Roger Rabbit* (1988), *Mermaids* (1990), *Hook* (1991) and *Nixon* (1995). Joanne Whalley's career took off with the acclaimed television serials *Edge of Darkness* (1985) and *The Singing Detective* (1986). She seemed on the verge of movie stardom after *Willow* (1988) and *Scandal* (1989). Moving to Hollywood, Whalley marked time in *Navy SEALS* (1990) and *Shattered* (1991), which also starred Bob Hoskins. Bob Geldof played another lead role in *Number One* (1985), which blended romance, villainy and snooker against an East End backdrop. Cast as Harry 'Flash' Gordon, Geldof was supported by a strong cast, including Alison Steadman, Phil Daniels, Alfred Molina, Ian Dury, Ray Winstone and Alun Armstrong. Scripted by acclaimed writer GF Newman, *Number One* proved uneven. The well drawn characters and subplots were undermined by the unconvincing snooker sequences. Released in the UK in March 1985, the film did poorly at the box-office. Three years on from *The Wall*, Geldof's name meant little in the United States and *Number One* went straight to the small screen. Having waived his salary for a share of the profits, Geldof got little out of the film and his acting career stalled. In any event, Geldof's life soon took a radically different direction. Appalled by images of starving children in Ethiopia, Geldof recruited most of Britain's pop talent for the charity single 'Do They Know It's Christmas?' The following year, Geldof organised the landmark benefit concert Live Aid (1985).

In 1983, Thorn-EMI released *Pink Floyd The Wall* on videocassette. In line with industry practices, the 2.35:1 aspect ratio was cropped to a TV-friendly 1.33:1, losing nearly half the original widescreen image. Despite this compromise, *The Wall* proved a big hit on video. According to Roger Waters, the movie was better suited to the videotape medium than the big screen, in many ways. Interviewed by Ray White, he explained: '…it's so successful on video 'cause you don't have to watch the whole thing. You can watch your favourite bits or you can fast forward… you don't have to sit there and be bombarded with this unremitting assault on the senses, like you had to in the cinema.'

For copyright reasons, this initial video release was deleted after a short period. In the mid-1980s, *The Wall* became one of the most requested videos. Stores put up signs announcing the film was unavailable, alongside two other cult musicals, *The Rocky Horror Picture Show* (1975) and *The Blues Brothers* (1980). In 1987, *The Wall* was finally re-released, by Cannon Screen Entertainment, using the same full-screen transfer as the Thorn-EMI version. *The Wall* was reissued by Channel 5 – not connected with the TV network – in 1990.

In the United States, MGM/UA released *The Wall* on video and laserdisc in 1983. Both formats featured a pan and scan version of the film. Retailing at $34.98, the laserdisc only beat the video on sound quality, with Dolby surround. According to some sources, the full-screen laserdisc version was also released in Germany, in 1990. Distributed by Polygram, the disc sold for 59 Deutschmarks, around £25. In September 1991, MGM/UA released a letterboxed collector's edition. The disc also offered Dolby surround sound, both digital and analogue, and a theatrical trailer. MGM/UA gave this letterboxed version a simultaneous video release. In July 1997, *The Wall* was reissued on laserdisc in an extra special edition, retailing at $39.98. This director-approved, THX-mastered letterboxed version had enhanced Dolby surround sound, based on the six-track recording used for the 70mm theatrical release. The disc also featured a photo gallery, trailer and running commentary by Alan Parker. For licensing reasons, this release was limited to one pressing, quickly going out of print. While laserdisc is now an obsolete format, copies of the *deluxe* edition are still highly sought after, selling for £20 or more.

In 2000, Sony Music Video gave *The Wall* a definitive release in the DVD format, available across Region 1, 2 and 4 territories. The disc featured a new Hi Definition film transfer, from the original anamorphic interpositive, and remastered 5.1 Dolby Digital and Surround Encoded PCM Stereo Soundtracks, made from the original master tapes. The numerous extras include the deleted 'Hey You' sequence, which had acquired semi-legendary status. In 1990, Roger Waters tried to locate the footage, only to be told that the original film elements – the negative and interpositive – had been destroyed. The DVD presented 'Hey You' as a scratched, black and white work print, presumably the only surviving version. While many shots from the sequence appeared elsewhere in *The Wall*, reassembling them for the DVD would have been time-consuming and expensive. Alongside the urban rioting and police clashes, the 'Hey You' montage offered Pink's naked wife and yet more maggots. Aside from the usual trailer and production stills, the DVD included the 'Another Brick in the Wall' promo shot for *Top of the Pops* and *The Other Side of the Wall*. The disc also featured a new, two-part retrospective documentary, *Looking Back at the Wall*, produced and directed by Storm Thorgerson and Bob Bentley. The 45 minute *Looking Back* special included contributions from Roger Waters, Gerald Scarfe, Alan Parker, Alan Marshall, Peter Biziou and James Guthrie. For all the production strife, Parker claimed to be 'proud' of his contribution to the movie. Scarfe admitted to being puzzled by *The Wall*'s enduring cult success: 'I'm not sure what people get from it.'

Regrettably, the DVD didn't include the Alan Parker commentary recorded for the 1997 US laserdisc release. Presumably, this was down to copyright problems with MGM/UA. However, the disc featured a new commentary, recorded by Roger Waters and Gerald Scarfe. Though somewhat patchy, their comments proved of considerable interest. Scarfe concedes that *The Wall* has a 'slightly misogynistic' element, accepting his share of the blame. While Waters and Scarfe refer to the clashes with Alan Parker, they say relatively little about him. Scarfe claims the three-way collaboration began well, before both he and Waters fell out with Parker: 'It was a bit of a struggle, really, most of it.' In the interests of diplomacy, Scarfe doesn't blame Parker in particular: 'We were all used to getting our own way in our own fields…we were all elbowing and muscling one another out.' Scarfe even saw a positive side to this three-way conflict: 'There was a certain amount of angst, which reflects itself in the film, perhaps successfully.' That said, the implication remains that Parker was the real 'problem' on the film.

Elsewhere, Waters has damned the director with faint praise: 'Alan Parker is an extremely accomplished technician.' By contrast, Waters describes Peter Biziou as a 'great' director of photography. Waters also praises Bob Geldof's performance as Pink: 'I thought he was very good.' Waters seems unfazed by Geldof's lack of appreciation for the music: 'Not everybody can be a Pink Floyd fan.' Waters shows off his humorous Irish accent, presumably not a personal dig at Geldof. There are also discussions about psychotherapy, institutional racism in the UK police force, and the nature versus nurture aspect of child abuse. Discussing the much-debated ending, Waters saw the child who dismantles the Molotov cocktail as 'rejecting the folly of the previous generation'. There is hope for the world, after all, rebuilt outside the shadow of The Wall.

Two decades on, *Pink Floyd The Wall* remains a major cult phenomenon. Images from *The Wall* have appeared on T-shirts, rolling papers, wristwatches, fridge magnets and belt buckles. A number of Gerald Scarfe's animated characters – notably the bum-faced judge, bug-eyed teacher and marching hammer – were issued as limited edition plastic figures. Fans who collected the complete set could also build their own miniature Wall backdrop. For all the creative differences and ego clashes, the *Wall* movie has a raw power that transcends its production problems and inherent flaws. Interviewed for the DVD release, Alan Parker summed up the essence of *Pink Floyd The Wall*: 'At the heart of it is Roger's primal scream. It's Roger's piece and it's Roger's madness.'

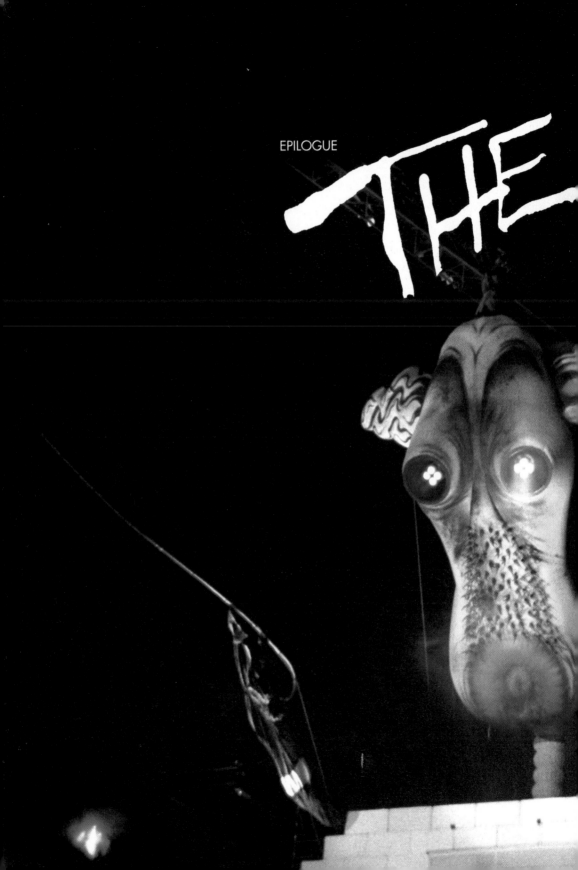

EPILOGUE THE

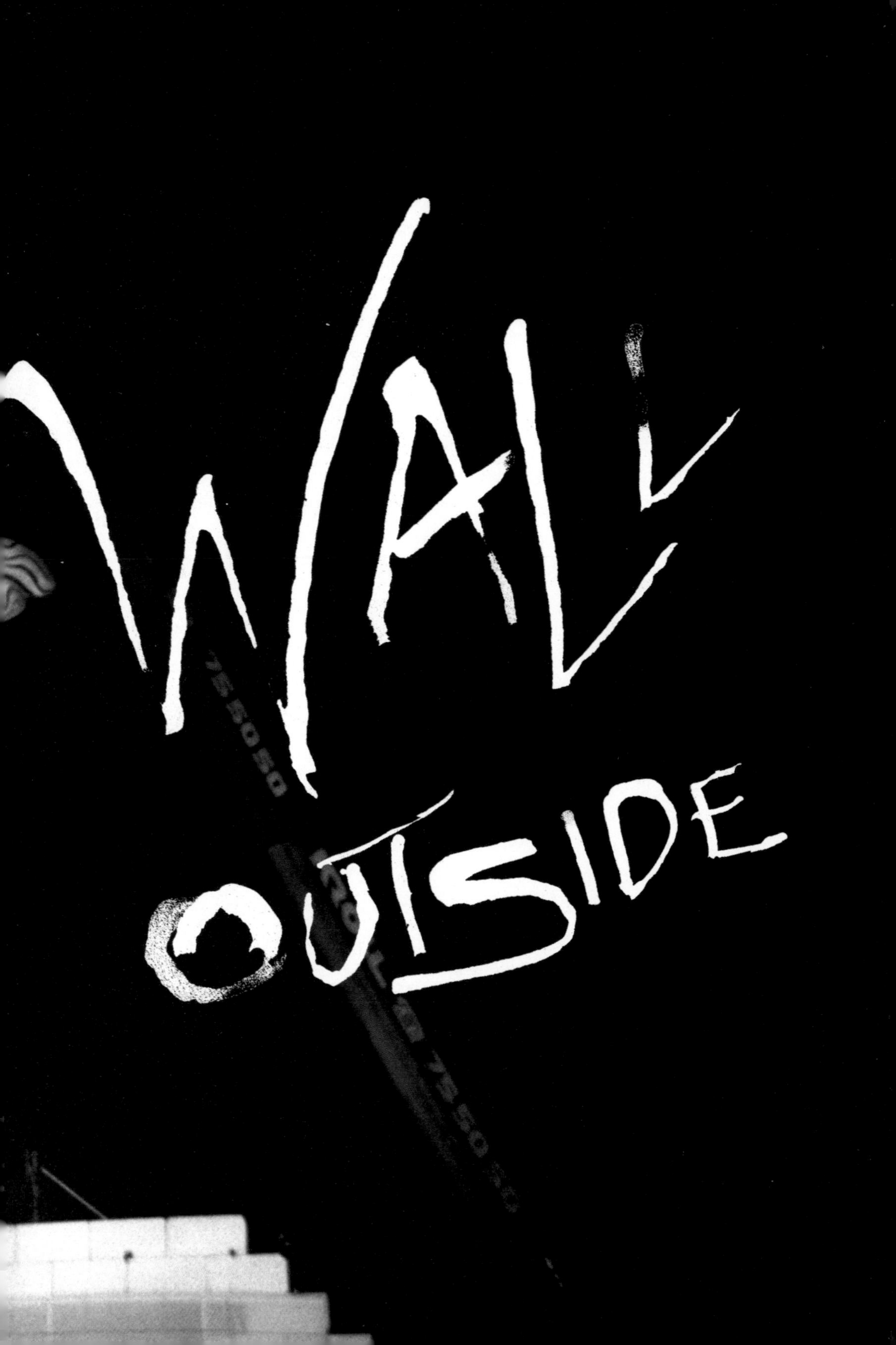
WALL
OUTSIDE

The fragmentation of Pink Floyd continued throughout the recording of *The Final Cut*, the follow-up to *The Wall*, in 1982. *The Final Cut* was a Roger Waters solo album in all but name (David Gilmour had his name removed from the production credits) and marked what many believed to be the closing chapter in the band's turbulent history. Waters resigned from the group in 1985, confidently expecting the name Pink Floyd to quietly retire. By 1986, however, a bitter legal wrangle had developed between Waters on one side and Gilmour and Mason on the other. Gilmour and Mason pressed ahead with a new Floyd album (ultimately reinstating Rick Wright, lending extra credence to their use of the group's name) and Waters' attempts to prevent them recording and touring ultimately proved fruitless.

With his legal efforts stymied, Waters felt confident that the public would recognise *his* claim to the Pink Floyd legacy, but in the album charts and concert arenas of 1987 Pink Floyd's *A Momentary Lapse of Reason* beat Waters' *Radio KAOS* hands down. Waters famously dismissed *A Momentary Lapse of Reason* as 'a pretty fair forgery', and was bemused by what he felt to be a lack of recognition for his contribution to Pink Floyd's (now ongoing) success.

It was during this relatively unfulfilling period in Waters' solo career that he first toyed with the idea of performing *The Wall* as a solo show. The project was conceived as a benefit for The Memorial Fund For Disaster Relief, a new charity established by Group Captain Leonard Cheshire VC. Although Cheshire's musical tastes leaned more towards big band music than rock and roll, he recognised that the new charity – which aimed to amass a £500 million trust fund to alleviate international disasters – would benefit from being launched at a high profile event, and that the revenue from ticket sales and merchandise could help kick start the fund.

Working with Jonathan Park, Waters considered numerous venues for the new presentation, including Red Square, the Sahara Desert, Monument Valley and Wall Street. When, after years of speculation, demolition of the Berlin Wall began in November 1989, the perfect venue seemed to present itself. It seemed 'completely obvious' to Waters to stage *The Wall* on the site, and preparations for the ambitious show began.

'In the hurry and scurry of it all coming together we didn't really think whether we were right or whether we were appropriate,' says the show's producer Tony Hollingsworth. 'We could see that there was this very direct, simple, analogy between *The Wall* and the wall, and that one dealt with personal alienation and that one dealt with political alienation, and no-one went any further than that into the appropriateness of the creativity.'

The outdoor concert would climax with the poignant demolition of a 60-foot wall. The stage would be constructed at the Potsdamer Platz, the former no-man's land that

The latest incarnation of Pink Floyd was unveiled in 1986. The group now comprised Nick Mason, David Gilmour and the reinstated Rick Wright.

once divided Berlin with a wall to the east and a wall to the west. Information about the barren patch of land inbetween was sketchy, and a thorough search using minesweepers revealed a number of buried grenades. The search also uncovered the SS bunker in which Adolf Hitler had spent his final days.

The event would be the biggest concert ever staged on German soil. One British newspaper estimated the total production cost at £7.5 million, although it was anticipated that these overheads would be recouped from the sale of rights to the 100 television stations screening the live performance around the world.

Although many critics and reporters mistakenly previewed the event as a Pink Floyd concert, Waters was adamant that he would perform the piece solo, albeit in the company of a number of special guests. 'Mr Mason and Mr Gilmour I doubt will receive an invitation,' he

Ute Lemper (as Pink's wife) and Jerry Hall (as the groupie) join a triumphant Roger Waters on stage at Berlin

said prior to the concert. 'Philosophically, politically, physically and musically we no longer share a point of view. I have no more respect for them.'

Recruiting celebrity musicians proved to be less than straightforward, however – Eric Clapton (who had accompanied Waters when he toured his 1984 release *The Pros and Cons of Hitchhiking*), Joe Cocker, Bob Dylan, Peter Gabriel and Rod Stewart all proved unavailable. The songs from *The Wall* would ultimately be re-interpreted by artists that included The Scorpions ('In The Flesh'), Cyndi Lauper ('Another Brick in the Wall part 2'), Sinead O'Connor ('Mother'), Joni Mitchell ('Goodbye Blue Sky'), Bryan Adams ('Young Lust') and Van Morrison ('Comfortably Numb'). 'The Trial' would be brought to life by Thomas Dolby as the schoolmaster, Ute Lemper as Pink's wife, Marianne Faithfull as Pink's mother, Tim Curry as the prosecutor and Albert Finney as the judge. Waters' backing group for the entire performance included Snowy White and Peter Wood, who had been among Pink Floyd's supplemental musicians at the Earl's Court shows.

Following a filmed dress rehearsal on Friday 20 July 1990, the gates were opened to allow the first ticket-holders into the site the following afternoon. As the day progressed it became clear that so many people had arrived to watch the show that shutting them out would present a health and safety risk. The ultimate audience number is estimated at approximately 350,000 – records aren't precise because only the first 250,000 were charged entry to the concert.

Waters' return to open-air performances was staged in elaborate and bombastic style. New inflatables included a giant, black pig, and a 120-foot high teacher. 'I didn't feel any ambivalence about doing the show outdoors,' Waters told *Rolling Stone* after the concert. 'My feeling is that the young people in Germany are much closer to themselves, and their feelings, than the young people were in the Olympic Stadium in Montreal… In Montreal they were thinking, "Hey, where's the fucking beer tent?" – and really, as far as I could tell, very little else.'

A number of technical problems threatened the show during its earliest stages. Problems with circuit breakers meant that power was cut to the stage during 'The Thin Ice' and 'Mother' (in the agonising minutes following the latter breakdown, a desperate Waters resorted to entertaining the audience and television viewers by tap-dancing). Footage from the dress rehearsal, and a subsequent partial re-staging, was substituted in the video and DVD releases of the concert.

Following the demolition of the wall, Waters led the company in a rendition of 'The Tide Is Turning', the outstanding track from *Radio KAOS*, and a less ambivalent

135

optimistic statement than 'Outside the Wall', the track that originally closed *The Wall*.

Critical reaction to the concert was mixed, and its corresponding live album made little impact on the charts (number 27 in the UK and number 57 in the US). Waters was justifiably proud of his achievement, amusingly self-deprecating about the technical problems, and critical of certain aspects of the show (he remains vociferous about Sinead O'Connor's attitude on the night and her subsequent behaviour).

Despite its high profile, the Berlin show ultimately did little to boost Waters' solo career. His 1992 solo album *Amused To Death* was the finest he had recorded to date but, perhaps mindful of the difficulties he had faced in the late 1980s, Waters decided not to tour. Gilmour, Mason and Wright returned with their latest Pink Floyd album, *The Division Bell*, in 1994. A markedly superior and more cohesive effort than *A Momentary Lapse of Reason*, the album and subsequent tour were huge commercial successes. Tracks such as 'Poles Apart' and 'Lost For Words' may have been veiled references to the estranged Waters, but the album's elegiac air suggested that the disoute was about to become largely academic. 'I don't think about it,' said Gilmour in 2003, when asked whether there would ever be another Pink Floyd album. 'It's not anywhere in my list of things I ought to think about. It just isn't relevant at this stage and I have no inclination to think about it.' When pressed about Roger Waters, Gilmour claims, 'I don't really have any feelings about him.'

In 1999 Roger Waters embarked on a tour that marked a spectacular return to prominence. In recent years he has performed numerous live dates and, in June 2002, played two shows at London's Wembley Arena. At both nights, Waters was joined on stage by Nick Mason, who added his drums to an emotional performance of 'Set The Controls For The Heart Of The Sun'. The tour also included renditions of *Wall* songs such as 'Mother', 'Comfortably Numb' and, inevitably, 'Another Brick in the Wall part 2'. In common with the much less successful Pink Floyd tour of 1977, Waters' recent shows have all been performed under the title 'In The Flesh'.

In the sleeve notes of Waters' latest live album, also entitled *In The Flesh*, he admits to 'a fundamental change in my attitude towards what I do... Much of this has to do with understanding, or I should rather say, feeling, the truly reciprocal nature of the arrangements between me and my audiences.' To construe Waters' reconciliation with Nick Mason as the first step towards a Pink Floyd reunion would probably be a mistake, but it would seem that he has finally found a sense of closure on the events triggered by the incident at the Olympic Stadium. The wall that once separated Roger Waters from his audiences has, it seems, finally been demolished.

BIBLIOGRAPHY

Aizlewood, John, 'I Won't Be Drawn On That', *Q*, November 1994

Alvarez, A (ed), *The New Poetry*, Penguin, 1962

Anderson, Pete and Watkins, Mike, *Crazy Diamond: Syd Barrett and the Dawn of Pink Flo* Omnibus Press, 1991, 1993

Black, Johnny, 'The Long March', *Mojo*, November 2001

Boucher, Caroline, 'Waters in the Pink...', *Disc and Music Echo*, 8 August 1970

Carr, Ian, *Miles Davis*, Paladin, 1984

Clerk, Carol, 'Lost In Space', *Uncut*, June 2003

Dallas, Karl, *Bricks In The Wall*, SPI Books, 1987, 1994

Dellar, Fred, 'So Wrong, Yank Floyd Alight', *Mojo*, February 2004

Denselow, Robin, 'The Floyd's tour de force' *The Guardian,* 22 July 1988

Easlea, Daryl, 'David Gilmour', *Record Collector*, May 2003

Fricke, David, 'Pink Floyd – the inside story', *Rolling Stone*, 19 November 1987

Graustark, Barbara and Huck, Janet, 'Up against the wall', *Newsweek*, 10 March 1980

Henderson, Peter and Sutcliffe, Phil, 'The First Men on the Moon', *Mojo*, March 1998

)ert, Tom, 'Who the hell does Roger Waters think he is?', *Q*, November 1992

ibet, Andy; MacDonald, Bruno; Walker, Dave & Carole (eds), *The Amazing Pudding: Original Pink Floyd and Roger Waters Magazine*

:Donald, Bruno (ed), *Pink Floyd Through The Eyes of...*, Sidgwick & Jackson, 1996

:Donald, Ian, *Revolution in the Head: The Beatles' Records and the Sixties*, rth Estate, 1994, 1997

es, Barry, *Bob Dylan: In His Own Words*, Omnibus Press, 1978

es, Barry, *Pink Floyd: A Visual Documentary*, Omnibus Press 1980, 1988

icios, Julian, *Lost In The Woods: Syd Barrett and The Pink Floyd*, Boxtree, 1998

erson, Richard and Samuelson, David W, 'Notes on *Pink Floyd The Wall*', *erican Cinematographer*, October 1982

tress, Mark, 'Screamadelica', *Mojo Collections*, Spring 2001

ey, Glenn (ed), *Brain Damage: The Pink Floyd, Waters & Barrett Magazine*

ey, Glenn and Russell, Ian, *Pink Floyd: In The Flesh*, Bloomsbury, 1997

dall, Robert, 'The Third Coming', *Mojo*, May 1994

affner, Nicholas, *Saucerful of Secrets: The Pink Floyd Odyssey*, Sidgwick & Jackson, 1991

imons, Sylvie, 'Danger! Demolition In Progress', *Mojo*, December 1999

cliffe, Phil, 'The 30 Year Technicolour Dream', *Mojo*, July 1995

lker, Alexander, *National Heroes: British Cinema in the Seventies and Eighties*. Harrap, 1986

Walsh, John, 'Here We Go, Here We Go, Here We Go', *Q*, November 1994

Waters, Roger (lyrics), *Pink Floyd The Wall*, Avon, 1982

Welch, Chris, 'Chris Welch finds out what Britain's top "overground" group are planning', *Melody Maker*, 3 May 1969

Welch, Chris, 'Floyd Joy', *Melody Maker*, 19 May 1973

PICTURE CREDITS

Front cover: London Features International/Rex Features
Back cover: Retna

Rex Features: pages 15, 17, 19, 21, 23, 27, 31, 35, 39, 47, 52, 55, 75, 79, 80, 84, 86, 87, 94, 99, 134
The Joel Finler Collection: pages 90, 102, 104, 108, 111, 112, 115, 116, 119, 121, 122 (*Pink Floyd The Wall* © MGM/UA Entertainment Co)
London Features International: pages 42, 45, 49, 50, 57, 59, 63, 64, 88
Matt Johns: pages 60, 82, 83, 100, 130, 135, 137, 138
Ian McKenzie: pages 7, 9, 85
Retna: pages 53, 54, 61
Marcus Hearn: page 2

Our special thanks to Matt Johns (www.brain-damage.co.uk) and Ian McKenzie for their assistance with picture research.